Golf à la Carte

Golf à la Carte

The Best of Dobereiner

Peter Dobereiner

Illustrations by John Ireland

Lyons & Burford, Publishers

Printed in the United States of America

10 9 8 7 6 5 4 3 2

Library of Congress Cataloging-in-Publication Data

Dobereiner, Peter.
    Golf à la carte : the best of Dobereiner / Peter Dobereiner ;
illustrations by John Ireland.
        p.   cm.
    ISBN 1-55821-145-4
    1. Golf.   2. Golf—Humor.   I. Title.
GV967.D626   1992
796.352'0207—dc20   92-2
                                                             CIP

First published in Great Britain by Stanley Paul, Ltd.

Contents

Introduction

During the 30 years I have devoted to writing about golf I reckon that I have learnt something new about the game every single day. That means that as recently as 10 years ago there were 3,650 pieces missing from the jigsaw puzzle of my knowledge. Even making allowances for inconsequential items of information, those tiresome plain blue pieces which form the sky for the puzzle, this represents a veritable encyclopaedia of ignorance. This is one reason why I wish that everything I have ever written on the subject of golf could be gathered up and incinerated. Most of it has been burnt, of course, for such is the perishable nature of newspaper and magazine writing that it is fit only for the next day's bonfire. But specimens always escape the cleansing flame as yellowing cuttings to mock the author's vanity. And that same vanity cannot resist the flattering suggestion that the survivors might make a book. So bang goes yet another piece of the rain forest. I am indebted to *Golf Digest, Golf World, The Observer, The Guardian* and *Homes Abroad* for permitting a new lease of life to this selection of articles and hope that some of the pleasure I had in writing them will be regenerated in the reading.

Peter Dobereiner

Chapter 1

What is this thing called golf?

Back in the cave age

Scientists who search for the origin of man work to a time-honoured formula. The newly graduated anthropologist departs for East Africa and spends 20 years grubbing around in the dirt with a trowel until finally, with a Neanderthal grunt of triumph, he rises to his feet holding a minute splinter of fossilized shinbone.

This he carefully traces on a large sheet of paper and then, from his vast knowledge and experience, he outlines with a dotted line the silhouette of the creature that originally owned that bit of bone. Invariably, this reconstruction turns out to resemble a naked golfer strolling down a fairway.

The scientist now has to ask himself the vital question: Was this creature a man or an ape? There are certain standard tests to determine the answer. Did it possess the power of reason? Did it communicate by speech? Did it have a sense of humour?

My own brilliant contribution to this scientific discipline has been to devise a vastly simplified system of distinguishing man from ape. All the scientist has to do is ask one straightforward question: Could this creature have played golf?

You can perhaps guess the line of research that I am now pursuing. Most scientists accept that the origin of our species occurred along the pattern laid down by Charles Darwin, namely that sometime, for some reason, an ape decided to stand on his back legs and walk erect, thereby becoming a man.

That is fine as far as it goes but the theory begs the central question of why an ape should suddenly decide to stand up. I am a committed Darwinian but I prefer Bernard to Charles. My theory is that there was only one possible reason for an ape to stand up on his hind legs: to play golf.

Imagine our original ancestor, when in his ape form, moving on all fours along a jungle track. A small armadillo runs out and stops in terror, rolling itself into a perfect sphere for protection. The ape, equally taken aback, grabs a stick and whacks at the creature. The armadillo describes a perfect parabola through the air, lands on a grassy glade, takes two hops forward and then checks under the influence of backspin and rolls slowly into a rabbit hole.

Another ape, witnessing this scene, snatches the wretched armadillo from the hole, grabs the stick and tries to emulate that remarkable ace. The ape family is notorious for its penchant for imitation; it would be irresistible for the second ape. Thus golf was born.

Now, with the rudimentary game established, the way was open for the birth of mankind and the dawn of civilization. The apes had to learn to walk upright. They also had to learn how to fashion golf clubs, variations of which were used for hunting. The power of reason developed with succeeding generations so that these primitive golfers could decide on club selection, read borrows in the greens and work out the bets.

As night follows day, those first men would have had to devise a means of spoken communication, if only to tell each other lies about how they would have broken 70 had a passing brontosaurus not deflected the ball on the last green. So Homo became Homo sapiens and the way was cleared for man to conquer the earth and, in due course, the heavens. We have golf to thank for Shakespeare's sonnets and Rembrandt's portraits.

However, if we observe life in a cosmic context, we see that everything goes in cycles. Plants emerge in spring, flourish, and wither in the fall, then lie dormant before the process begins again. We humans are born, struggle to get down to single-figure handicaps and then return to the earth, which gave us our being. We tend to accept that the civilizing process of man will continue forever, in a steadily rising graph of progress. Be warned. There is evidence to suggest that the process that produced man from ape is itself a cycle. The process of decay is evident in the same sphere that started it all: golf.

Let us go back to those original definitions of man and see how our modern pro golfers measure up.

The power of reason: apart from Jack Nicklaus, and to a lesser degree Tom Watson, this faculty seems to be disappearing.

Sense of humour: totally vanished from the world of golf except for Lee Trevino.

Ability to speak: here we have the hard evidence. 'I played super but potted mediocre.' That is the standard response of golfers today. The adverb has vanished from the vocabulary of golf. Other parts of speech are falling into disuse, as in the expression, 'I tripled five.'

On the golf course the players communicate in grunts. In the space of 18 holes a player may utter no more than half a dozen words: 'Yer up.' 'Short.' 'I'll finish.' ''Joyed it.'

I do not know whether it is possible to arrest this regression to the cave age, but I do feel we should try. Unless something is done – and quickly – it seems that by the next century man will drop down onto all fours again. And, quite possibly, start growing a tail.

Golf World, 1982

Golf's mitigating circumstances

'Having been convicted of murder after what I must say has been a very fair trial, I am most grateful to you, your honour, for your invitation to address the court before sentence is passed upon me.

Until the fateful day in question I had been aware of the victim only as the epicentre of a rowdy crowd of salesmen, medical persons and stockbrokers who habitually monopolise the far corner of the clubhouse bar for the exchange of stories of dubious taste.

Our formal meeting was thus on the first tee for our first-round confrontation in the club seniors' knockout cup. He had his arms entwined around his driver which he held across the small of his back and he was making writhing movements which I can only describe as resembling the death throes of a harpooned fish. Having disentangled himself from this unfortunate predicament, he teed his ball and went into a complicated ritual of standing behind it and looking up the fairway as if observing it for the first time in his life, wrapping each finger of his left hand one by one around the grip of his driver in accordance with a pattern he had painted on the rubber surface and then carefully placing the clubhead behind the ball.

He then went into a slow-motion flamenco dance while swishing his imaginary tail like an excited spaniel puppy. Having satisfied himself that he had achieved a satisfactory position for his feet, he completed the process by slowly and reverentially placing his right hand on the club in the manner of a bishop blessing a confirmation candidate. There then followed a longish pause, broken by a series of convulsions in which he appeared to be breaking invisible bonds which prevented him from taking the club back. He then slowly raised the club and hit the ball gently wide of the ladies' tee.

'You saw what I did?' he inquired in the urgent tones of a fanatic.

'Yes,' I replied with as much civility as I could muster. 'You hit it into those bushes.'

'No, no! I crossed the line.' He raised his arms and held the position at the top of the backswing, craning his neck to observe the set of his wrists and the angle of the club-face. 'You see, the club is laid off. From here you shatter Ben Hogan's pane of glass.' He made a minute adjustment and completed the swing. 'That's how it should be done.' He made another full swing. 'That one would have gone straight up the middle because the club is on the true swingplane.'

When he eventually played his second shot after five rehearsals, he hoiked the ball into the pond behind the fifth green, conceded the hole and gave me the benefit of his instant analysis. 'I hit early. Good pronation going back but I slightly rushed the supination phase. This game's all about timing. Golf should be played to the tempo of an old-fashioned waltz.'

To my inner consternation, he actually sang during his next tee shot. Having gone through his full rigmarole of addressing the ball, he suddenly burst into a fruity baritone rendition. 'Da da dee dee dum (top of backswing) dum dum (end of weight shift and hip slide) dum damn.'

The reason for that improvised final syllable was that at the moment of what should have been impact the ball completely disappeared. We stood mystified. After what seemed like an age there was a loud plop as his ball, falling vertically from an enormous height, landed 50 yards ahead of us.

'Went clean under it,' he said. 'No release. With the straight-faced driver you have to hit slightly on the upswing, but because I did not release as I came into the impact area the clubhead continued on its downward arc and went under the ball.'

The rest of the round was a continuation of my opponent's expert litany, but by calling upon all my reserves of self-control, your honour, I refrained from cleaving his skull with my pitching wedge and, in accordance with the honoured conventions of this great game, we repaired to the bar afterwards. I ordered a very stiff one but I cannot claim that my subsequent actions were influenced by alcohol.

At this point my opponent was joined by his usual cronies and he immediately launched into a shot-by-shot description of his round, complete with actions, detailed descriptions of the flight of the ball and his expert analysis of what he had done wrong.

Ten minutes later, on the second hole, something snapped inside my brain. To my horror I observed my right hand, acting under its own volition, rise slowly and tip an entire bottle of powerful analgesic tablets into his drink. (I carry these as I am subject to occasional migraine headaches.) You know the rest of the story. I am now ready to suffer the full penalty of the law which your honour may deem fit to visit upon me for my vile crime.'

The judge, however, who had a curiously white, almost bleached, left hand, pronounced the sentence, but it was some time before I was able to take in the import of what he had said: 'Due to overwhelming mitigating circumstances the prisoner is discharged on condition that he gives an undertaking to be of good behaviour in future.'

Golf World, 1989

Read between the lines on the forehead

The PGA Championship is more than a golf tournament; it is a major sporting event, like Super Bowl or the Kentucky Derby, and as such it will attract thousands of spectators who will not be familiar with the finer points of the game.

My purpose is not to describe how the game is played or to explain the rules, for the first is obvious and the second is impossible, but to offer a little guidance on the behaviour of the players. Watching them on the course and reading their comments in the newspapers, you might well get the impression that they are insane. In a strictly clinical sense, that is by no means true in every case. The fact is that they are all in the grip of dark and mysterious forces; they are the hapless victims of what they believe to be an evil spirit.

Of course, that is superstitious nonsense. The idea of malicious spirits died with the witches of Salem and has no place in the latter part of the twentieth century, although golfers are reluctant to accept it. The plain fact is that there are natural laws which affect us all, as the sage Christopher Stuart enunciated way back in 1752 in the following rhyme:

'I never had a piece of toast
Particularly long and wide
But fell upon the sanded floor,
And always on the buttered side.'

You know the way these natural laws work. Any time someone offers you a fruit-flavoured Lifesaver, there is always one of those horrible green ones at the top of the roll. Twenty minutes before a girl's first date, she develops a pimple. That's not the work of evil spirits; that's life. Golf is a part of life, and I have spent many years isolating and codifying the natural laws as they apply to golf.

Let us start with a few simple examples.

Besselink's Law: 'All trees are magnetic.'

That one explains itself and it is closely allied to **Newton's Variation**. This is rather more tricky. You must understand that all the competitors this week have measured the golf course and know to the inch how far it is to the flag on every shot. They also know, pretty well to the inch, how far they hit the ball with any given club. Therefore, since they are all highly skilled players, every shot ought to go exactly the correct distance. Well, find a comfortable seat behind the 18th green and observe one of golf's more important natural laws, because **Newton's Variation** states: 'The distance a golf ball will travel is proportional to the mass of the clubhead and the square of its speed, *except over water*.' A proper understanding of that law will do much to explain the irrational behaviour of the players, such as kicking their caddies, beating the ground with their clubs, and baying like a wolf under a full moon.

Now for a few more obvious ones.

Weiskopf's Locker Room Assertion: 'When you are late for your tee time, you always break a shoelace.'

Bolt's Syndrome: 'The key shot in any round can only be played with the club you wrapped around the tree three holes back.'

Trevino's Truism: 'It's an ill wind that blows up the minute you nominate a high-trajectory ball.'

Crenshaw's Law of Universal Frustration: 'The one time you drive in the fairway, your ball winds up in a divot hole.'

Player's Platitude: 'Luck is something enjoyed by the other guys.'

Nicklaus' Nostrum: 'Every time you have a six-footer to win a major championship, there's a patch of *poa annua* on the line.'

Watson's Wry Witticism: 'Dogs never bark on the follow-through.'

Hinkle's Hypothesis: 'Trees are 90 per cent air.'

To the spectator who is not conversant with the game of golf, the antics of the players on the greens may be perplexing. After all, as you know well from that time you played Krayzee Putting in Atlantic City with those nice people you met from Hoboken, putting is not all that difficult. You just grab that stick thing and whack the ball through the door of the windmill. Child's play.

So it is, in theory. Threading a needle is also easy. You just give the thread a lick of spit, concentrate for a second and the job is done. Well, in professional golf at this level, things are slightly different. Imagine, if you will, trying to thread a needle while standing on one leg on a tight-rope stretched across Niagara Falls and being shot at by crack snipers. That's about what it is like to try to hole a cross-hill six-footer in the PGA Championship. The sheer tension of the occasion has given us a whole lexicon of natural laws of putting. Space permits only a few.

Hogan's Law of Self-Delusion: 'Putting is 10 per cent agony and 90 per cent luck.'

Jacklin's Rule of Natural Injustice: 'The more important the putt, the less likely it is to drop.'

Mahaffey's Moan: 'Even if you read the break, the grain will get you.'

Aoki's Assertion: 'Onry way to make row putting score is to hit ball crose to frag.'

By now you will have realized that golf's natural laws are malign, which accords with **Beman's Theory of Bloody-Mindedness** ('The probability of anything happening on the golf course is in inverse ratio to its desirability'), more succinctly expressed in **Floyd's Fundamental Finding:** 'Everything is against us.'

However, this doctrine of total hostility has one important exception. It applies only to professional golf, for the exact corollary operates among amateur players, and this sole benevolent natural law is expressed in **Palmer's Presumption:** 'Pros always find a gap.' As you walk around the course, you will frequently come across players who have fallen victim to Besselink's Law and have hit into the trees. Notice them carefully, for in every instance there will be a narrow gap directly in line with the green through which the golfer can play a recovery shot. (In amateur golf, on the other hand, the ball invariably ends up slap behind the thickest tree in the woods, often tangled among roots.)

I mentioned earlier that a certain charity is necessary in interpreting the remarks of pro golfers as quoted in the newspapers. (Sensitive spectators are advised not to try to eavesdrop on comments made by players on the course. It is much the best policy to keep well out of earshot.) However, it is the practice at great tournaments like this one to invite players into the press room for interviews, and the papers will be full of their observations all this week. In reading what they have said, it's a good idea to bear in mind that there is a natural law governing golf comment. With what may be something of a presumption, I have given my own name to this law. **Dobereiner's Attribution of Adjectival Adjustment** says: 'It is impossible to interpret a golfer's remarks without knowing his score.'

Thus the expression 'A really good test of golf' means a club where the speaker holds the course record. Also the phrase 'Nothing but a **** cow pasture' is a course on which Dave Hill has missed the cut. Beware of the addendum 'of its kind' tacked onto the end of a description of a golf course. Example – Gary Player: 'This is the finest course I have ever seen, of its kind.' That translates as: 'The Commissioner has warned me that next time I criticize a host club in public he will have my guts for garters.'

I hope that this little dissertation has given you some small insight into professional golf and its special problems and that you will not rush to the conclusion that golfers are all dangerous lunatics. Be charitable and generous with your applause for their good shots. Of course, that raises the point that, as an infrequent golf spectator, you may not be able to distinguish the good shots from the ordinary, or

standard shot. Well, as a rough rule of thumb you can tell a good shot by the way the player holds the pose on his follow-through, standing as if sculptured by Michelangelo, with just a hint of a smile playing around the corner of his mouth. But observe his expression closely. If he holds that pose for longer than a minute or so, it may be because he is transfixed with horror. Notice if his nostrils are flaring and whether a muscle is twitching in his jaw. That is a sure sign that his internal pressure is building up to a critical level and an untimely burst of applause may just be enough to cause him to explode. If you can manage to distinguish between these two mental states and react appropriately, then I am sure that you will have an enjoyable week's golf-watching.

Golf Digest, 1979

Six steps to golfing maturity

There has never been a time when recruits to the game of golf had access to more advice and instruction. Magazines explain the rules and etiquette of golf and provide a comprehensive service of how to swing the club and plan your strategic progress round the course. At golf clubs junior programmes give the same service at a personal level. The Golf Foundation does a wonderful job in providing a sound introduction to golf in the schools. Hardly a week goes by without television putting on some form of golf programme. All of it useful instruction for the beginner. And yet it seems to me that there are serious gaps in the subjects which young golfers are taught and today I would like to offer a few insights which can otherwise be acquired only by hard and embarrassing experience.

Gambling

Golf is enhanced by a small flutter, just as a boiled egg is insipid without a pinch of salt. However, the rule is to make absolutely sure that you understand all the implications of the wager you are being offered before you agree to risk so much as a penny. Do not be shy about asking for full explanations of how the bet works and never hesitate for a moment to say so if you prefer to keep the wager small and simple. A casual remark of 'automatic presses, of course' can throw all your calculation out and you can wind up winning the match but losing money, and more money than you had imagined possible.

Rules

Very few people know the rules properly and you are surely among their number. Proceed with caution. If your ball lands in a place which entitles you to a free drop, confirm this procedure with your opponent or fellow competitor. If you observe someone in your group taking undue advantage of a rule, or following a wrong procedure, you may well be embarrassed and say nothing. You think to yourself that you can beat him whether he cheats or not and let him get on with it. That is not doing him any favours, or yourself. Do not say 'Hey you can't do that there here, you cheating so and so.' Carry a rule book in your bag and be diplomatic. It should be sufficient to remark: 'I thought the rule said you had to drop within two club lengths. Shall we check it?' Of course, if he is really cheating, like kicking his ball or improving his lie, then he knows that he is cheating. In that case the best thing is to say: 'I am sorry but if you are going to do that sort of thing I prefer not to play with you,' and walk in.

Clothing

Such is the power of advertising and television that many young golfers get the idea that it is impossible to play golf unless you are wearing a shirt with a natty motif on the breast, two-tone golf shoes and a left-hand glove. It may come as a shock but I have to insist that it is quite possible to play golf without buying any special clothing at all. In dry weather, rubber-soled shoes are actually better for your game (and for the greens) and a glove can actually hamper your progress as a golfer. Why do the pros take off their gloves to putt? In order to increase the sensitivity of their fingers. Why not maximize the sensitivity of your hands for all shots?

Equipment

Surprising as it may sound, it is quite possible to play well and score well with no more than about eight clubs in your bag. That way you save money on equipment, save money on a trolley and you actually become a better golfer.

Severiano Ballesteros learnt his golf playing round with only a three-iron and he could play to par using just that one club.

Do not get the idea that you are putting yourself at a disadvantage unless you use a first-grade golf ball. Until you have a handicap of single figures you will play just as well with a cheaper ball.

Etiquette

The one addition I would make to the sensible instructions in this section of the rule book is to make sure that you watch your opponent's (or partner's) ball and mark the spot carefully if it should land in trouble. When you are playing, it is a great comfort to know that those who are with you will extend the same courtesy to you since many shots are ruined by prematurely looking up to see where the ball is going. You want to be free to be able to watch the club-head right onto the ball, without worrying about losing the ball. Other people want this same assurance.

Post mortems

When a golfer has finished a round the most interesting subject in the whole world, or so it seems to him, is the incredible, earth-shaking nature of that round, or individual shots in it. After all, to the person who has just performed these feats, they provided emotional shocks of delight or despair of such intensity that obviously others would be only too happy to share the experience. Resist the temptation to pass on that treasury of fascinating adventure. Take it from me there is nothing, absolutely nothing, more boring than hearing about other people's golf. On that subject I am an expert because my job is to listen to golfers describing their rounds. These are the greatest players in the world and the stories they have to tell would boggle the mind, or so they think. Even they bore my tits off so what makes you think that I or anyone else is remotely interested in hearing how you hit a seven-iron to 6 inches or took six to get out of a bunker.

Golf is an intensely personal game. Keep it that way!

Golf World, 1981

Hope springs eternal!

Earlier this year Frank D. Tatum Jnr retired at the end of his two-year term as president of the United States Golf Association and he marked his departure with a speech revealing his philosophy of golf, the ideals which he had tried to uphold and his hopes for the future of the game.

It was an important statement and I believe that his views deserve the widest audience, if only to promote discussion. Of necessity I must paraphrase his remarks on each subject.

Winter rules

They should be abolished. The game was founded on the premise that wherever you hit the ball within bounds you played it from where it lay or suffered a penalty. What is wrong with that?

Course preparation

Heavily watered courses mean that too much of golf is played in the air. Soft fairways and holding greens rob golf of two vital elements – the necessity to calculate a good deal of bounce and roll into planning a shot, and the element of chance – that the bounce or roll may not come off as planned. The game has become a slog from one mushy lie to another.

Money

The essence of the game is being lost among statistics showing who won how much. There are risks in skilled young players growing up in an environment that is directed towards the singular objective of playing golf for money. A game which has so much to offer in being played for its own sake becomes something else as it evolves primarily into a medium for making money. The heart of the game is missing when it is played in that frame of mind.

Amateurism

The spirit as well as the concept of amateurism in golf needs all the nurturing we can give it. 'My experience with the inner workings of the administration of the game has confirmed not just the validity but also the critical importance of having knowledgeable, dedicated amateurs determine and interpret the Rules of Golf. This keeps the emphasis where it belongs – on the fundamental fact that golf is a game to be played for its own sake.

Television

TV's limitless potential in golf is not being used properly. A good deal has been done to improve telecasts; a lot more remains to be done if we are to realise what we should from this medium.

The rules

They have become too much like income tax regulations in the sense of governing the affairs of ordinary mortals with a complex set of provisions which too few of them understand. Somehow the considerable wit and wisdom of the legislators should be mobilised to organise the rules in a way that will encourage ordinary mortals to understand them.

Distance

Serious consideration should be given to further limitations on the golf ball specifications to reduce the distance it can be hit. With players able to hit the one-iron 230-plus yards and the three-wood 250-plus yards the need for the driver is reduced and its importance should be reaffirmed.

Electric golf carts

These abominations eliminate a vital part of golf which is walking the course with your companions; golf is a game of rhythm which is enhanced in its rhythmical character by walking; carts destroy the sense of communicating with nature, they are voracious consumers of energy, many foul the atmosphere, all clutter the scene. They chew up grass, frustrate proper course maintenance; they spawn vast areas of macadam paths which destroy the beauty of the scene and produce aberrational bounces and ridiculous rulings. They have brought about the demise of the caddie and the opportunity for youngsters, such as Ben Hogan, Byron Nelson and Walter Hagen, to develop and enrich the game. Playing from a cart is not golf and cannot be golf.

Powerful, passionate stuff, you will agree, but coming from someone of the experience and stature of Sandy Tatum these views deserve careful consideration by all people who love golf and want to preserve what is best in the game.

The only surprise in this assertion of a golfing creed is the omission of a fire and brimstone condemnation of what I believe to be the game's most serious problem: slow play. To be fair, his marvellous diatribe against motorised carts singled out one of the most pernicious causes of slow play in America but this disease of slow play seems to be becoming endemic in golf, even among those who follow Tatum's ideal of walking the course with a light bag slung across the shoulder.

I just hope that Tatum's successor as USGA president, Will Nicholson, will be fired with the same evangelical fervour as Tatum has been, and will fight these demons with no less spirit.

Golf World, 1980

Chapter 2

Life with the gladiators

The wandering vagabonds

Perhaps it is the advance of old age, just another symptom of the policemen looking younger, the traffic wardens prettier and the jokes in *Punch* getting even duller, but it seems to me that life on the golf circuit has lost some of its sparkle.

Inevitably, I suppose, with so much money at stake. The young pros are serious and a bit too dedicated for their own good, at times. There seem to be no characters coming into the game, not in the grand style of Max Faulkner or Tommy Bolt. Even the caddies have become as respectable as chartered accountants. It was not so long ago when the beer tents would be carpeted two deep with drunken caddies. These days they stand around discussing the movement of the stock market.

Will we ever again see the like of Mad Mac, for instance? He carried for Faulkner and would have made a splendid music-hall turn. Winter or summer, he wore a selection of top coats. Beneath these layers he sported several ties but no shirt. His speciality was a pair of opera glasses from which the lenses had long since vanished. He used to peer through this bizarre instrument at the line of a putt and then deliver solemn judgment: 'Hit it slightly straight, sir.'

And then there was Little Mac, who caddied for Dai Rees for some time and whom I was glad to see bobbing and weaving among the crowd at a recent tournament. Standing side by side, Little Mac made Dai Rees look like a giant and it did not take much beer to top up the wee fellow. And when he had his ration aboard, Little Mac feared no man. At the slightest provocation he would put up his fists and I imagine he took a bit of handling. It would be like fighting a frenzied garden gnome.

At the time when he was in his prime the travelling caddies were not too fussy about their sleeping arrangements. If they couldn't find a boarding house with a convenient back window they slept rough. One night Little Mac found the perfect spot. The tournament was over and he crept between the folds of a dismantled tent. Came the dawn and the contractor's men folded the tent and loaded it onto their lorry, with Little Mac still peacefully sleeping inside like the meat in a sausage roll.

The era of the vagabond caddie really ended with the Battle of the Nineteenth Hole, which I should explain is a pub at St Andrews. Two enterprising caddies went to Prestwick to meet the aircraft bringing over two famous American golfers. They politely touched their caps and announced boldly: 'We are your caddies.' They took charge of the bags.

However, on arrival at St Andrews the golfers discovered that two quite different caddies had been booked for them. The arrangements had been made some weeks in advance. So the men who had gone to Prestwick had to give up the bags and, at this late juncture, they were unable to find work for that week. They just had to sit this one out. Their hard-luck stories generated considerable sympathy among the fraternity of caddies and at the end of the tournament a meeting was held in the Nineteenth Hole.

'Brothers,' said the spokesman, 'through no fault of their own two of our colleagues have been unable to work this week. I would like to pass a motion through the chair that a collection be taken up forthwith on their behalf.' So saying, a hat was passed and generously filled. The two beneficiaries silently trousered the loot, too overcome to trust themselves to speak.

It was an incident to touch the heart. Who could fail to be moved by such an example of brotherhood? Who indeed? The caddies who had actually carried the Americans' bags slipped quietly into the night.

They presented themselves at the hotel of their employers and recounted the events of that evening.

'Since Americans are famed – and justly so – for their legendary generosity, we thought you would like to know of an act of generosity on our part. Those two poor caddies who met you at Prestwick will be all right after all. As you know, they had no work but we have seen to it that their wives and children shall not starve. From the generous fees which you paid us, we in our part have donated a proportion – a goodly proportion, even if we say so ourselves – to those two unfortunates. It matters not that our own families will have to subsist on potato stew. The bailiffs will just have to get on with their work. We shall all scrape by, somehow. The most important thing is that you shall not return to America with those two men on your consciences. We just wanted you to know, you being compassionate men and noted for your own generosity, even though the sums involved would seem so paltry to wealthy men like yourselves that you would not even notice it.'

'We are,' replied the golfers, 'duly moved, even unto tears, by this tale of charity. There is, however, one small point which you should know. Those two men who were unable to work did not go unrewarded. We paid them in full, at the top rates. Now be so kind as to get the hell out of here you conniving, cadging bums.'

The caddies returned to the Nineteenth Hole in pensive mood and in some haste. And when they told the assembled company what they had learned the room was filled with wrath. And flying bottles.

And boots. And fists. And when the dust finally settled no pane of glass remained intact in the windows. Life on the caddie circuit has never been the same since.

Golf World, 1984

The match is the thing

Today I must preface my remarks with a disclosure of interest, namely that stroke-play is my second favourite form of golf and by quite a long way.

It is not the play itself that puts me off, it is the task of marking a card. The act of gripping a pencil between thumb and forefinger creates a short circuit in my nervous system and this has the effect of cutting communications between the brain and the rest of my body.

I continue to hack away at the ball but it is pure reflex, like the frenzied flapping of a chicken whose head has been severed. My head observes these antics in a dispassionate objective manner as if they were being performed by a stranger. Just look at that pathetic oaf. Of course, the gruesome entertainment soon palls and the conscious part of my being is free to pursue its independent interests, such as making a mental note that the car needs servicing, wondering whether runner beans spiral up their strings in reverse rotation in Australia, whether indeed they have runner beans in Australia, and noting that for the second day in succession I have contrived to put on odd socks.

In a recent competition my lower half was crouched over a tricky six-footer with a double borrow and my mind was deeply engaged in trying to isolate the exact drink to complement the perfection of the day, a problem which would require a decision in about an hour's time. On the face of it this was a chilled Chablis sort of a day but, then again, a case could be made for lager. After all, four hours in the sun must have dehydrated that clown clutching the putter. On the other hand, lager would not be the best preliminary if a little wine was to be enjoyed with lunch. Grape and grain . . . Good heavens! The loony missed the hole by a foot.

The zombie body reached for the driver on the next tee, an act which I could have told it was absolutely guaranteed to deposit the ball deep into the woods on the left. So what? Maybe that dryness of the palate would react better to something tart. After all, a grease spot responds better to a teaspoonful of detergent than it does to a bucketful of water.

Tournament professionals do not share my feelings about stroke-play but the great mass of sensible golfers do, don't you? Ultimately, we pay the piper so I believe that we should have some small say in calling the tune. In short, let us have more match-play tournaments.

The Match-Play Championship has died for want of sponsorship. In 1982 the only major professional match-play event in Britain will be the Suntory at Wentworth, which is odd because this is by a long way the most successful sponsored promotion in the history of golf. The Ryder Cup match (roll on 1983) is second only in public appeal to the Open championship itself.

The Americans are rediscovering the appeal of match-play. The top 64 players from the 1981 money list will engage in a running match-play championship next year, with three matches a week being played on Tuesdays as a pipe-opener to the weekly Tour event. Details of the final have not yet been settled.

Whenever the subject of professional match-play is raised it is always said that television does not like this form of golf because of the uncertainty of the denouement occurring in range of static cameras. In these days of lightweight cameras that objection has surely lost most of its force. In any event, reluctant as I am to monkey with the traditional forms of the game, there are ways of preserving the element of grabbing at the throat and kicking each other in the guts, which is the essence of match-play, and still taking the matches to the last green.

This point was well made by a reader who analysed the last Ryder Cup match and came up with the result that the Americans won by 241½ to 215½ on a holes-won basis, which sounds much more respectable than the actual 18½ points to 9½ drubbing. It could have been even closer if every match had been fought out to the last green, not that I am suggesting that the Ryder Cup should depart from the purity of true match-play.

But a team match could very well be played by awarding one point for every hole won, with every match being played out over the full 18 holes and the scoreboard clicking away like a basketball score.

However, the glaring gap in our golfing calendar is an open match-play championship. Now that the Royal and Ancient golf club has established a promotional machine second to none, this would be the time to consider an open match-play championship, especially as most of the work would be done by other bodies.

It stands to reason that we would all have a go in a good cause. If scrubbers played off in club championships, with the winners joining Category One players in county championships, with winners joining exempt club professionals in national championships, with the winners joining exempt tournament players in the Open finals . . . yes, a million £5 entry fees at the very least.

Add in TV and film rights, hospitality centres, admission charges, programme profits, exhibition tent rentals, car park dues and you are beginning to rack up a useful income. I don't know what the R and A would do with the surplus but I daresay that they would find a worthy use for the cash. That side of it is unimportant; the main thing would be that the finest flowering of the game of golf would bloom in the land again.

The Observer, 1981

Sponsorship and all that!

The worst of the daily crisis was over. I had safely groped my way from my hotel room down to the intensive care unit but the strong black coffee had not yet percolated through to the control centre and switched on my essential life support systems. As I stood beside the first tee I was therefore not at my razor sharp best. A player walked past me onto the tee, greeting me with a kindly 'Good morning.' I responded with a reflex 'morning' and tried desperately to focus. I knew him well, a good player and a helluva nice chap. But what was his name? Automatically I glanced at his golf bag and with difficulty read the legend: DAVID LANGLEY EXHAUSTS AND TIRES.

Of course. 'Play well, David,' I said. He gave me an odd look and hit a high, looping fade deep into the woods. David Langley exhausts and tires . . . It was a curious and ruthlessly honest slogan to have printed on your bag, I thought. That's what is wrong with British golfers, they become exhausted and tired. No staying power. But why advertise this disability?

After another booster dose of coffee a thin trickle of blood began to seep through my brain and I realised that the player in question had

in fact been Andrew Chandler. I checked the starting sheet. Yes, there he was: Andrew Chandler (David Langley Exhausts and Tyres). So that was it, a commercial attachment, one of the proliferating examples of personal sponsorship of pro golfers by companies.

These days most of the players have advertising material on their bags. Kitchen Queen, Anglia Agricultural, Hermetite Products, Kwik Fit Holdings, Tallon Pens . . . Frankly I had never heard of any of them. That, of course, is the whole point. The idea of sponsoring a golfer is so that the public will get to hear about the sponsoring company and become familiar with the name.

Some of these sponsorships are excellent, more patronage really than a business deal. But there have been cases of sponsors putting players under such stringent contracts that they virtually became golfing slaves, winning big money but having to hand it over to their rapacious angels. I should add that the sponsors in these cases have been unscrupulous individual entrepreneurs and I have never heard of a reputable company bleeding a golfer in this way.

Certain questions have been exercising the European Tournament Players' Division of the PGA, with the result that a rule has been introduced requiring players to obtain official permission to display advertising material. The tournament director can forbid advertising which may embarrass a sponsor, a case in point being a ban on Dunhill-sponsored players wearing their company livery during the Benson and Hedges International.

For myself, I would like to see a further regulation in order to safeguard the players. It would be in everyone's interests if the ETPD insisted on approving the terms of all personal sponsorship contracts. Just because nobody has been bitten by a shark yet does not mean that it is safe to bathe in sponsorship waters.

The larger question is whether such sponsorships are beneficial to golf, whether they are in fact necessary. For the moment it must be said that tournament golf could not survive without outside support. Perhaps the top 30 in the order of merit table can win enough profit to live comfortably but the vast majority of tournament players have to supplement their incomes by one means or another.

Some of them spend their winters accumulating enough of a nest-egg to bankroll them through the season and very resourceful they are too. Keith Ashdown played the circuit on the strength of a close season stint as a waiter. Willie Milne worked on a North Sea oil rig and Peter Berry borrowed the cash to buy a derelict cottage and renovated it with his own hands. The South African Tertius Claassens dropped right out of golf for a year and sweated himself back into solvency as a welder.

All this shows admirable dedication but it also reveals a serious weakness in professional golf. The game must always be structured so that the best players prosper and the weaker ones go to the wall. It is a dog eat dog jungle of a profession and must remain so, for that competitive element is what produces the stars and golf needs stars to survive.

But it is not only the weak players who are having to drop off the circuit. Good players, tournament winners, men who are exempt because they are among the top 60 golfers, cannot make ends meet through prize winnings alone. Without the subsidy of commercial sponsorship they have to turn reluctantly to club jobs.

That is the justification for sponsorships. It is irrelevant whether they are good or bad for golf: they are necessary.

For the time being that is all that matters. But pro golf must develop to the point whereby the nucleus of its playing strength, say 60 to 80 of the leading golfers, can make a decent living by their golf alone.

Golf World, 1980

In search of perfection

Come to think of it, I have never seen a good round of golf. Those eight birdies in a row by Severiano Ballesteros in a forlorn attempt to add the Italian Open championship to his collection of national titles last week must have been an impressive run but I did not see it and, anyway, it was not a complete round.

Ballesteros is always likely to produce a burst of decent golf because he is one of the few players in the world who has the skill to match his willingness to suffer a double-bogey in his quest to score an eagle on every hole he plays. He produced the shots to support that laudable ambition for about nine holes in the 1980 Dutch Open at Hilversum. He could not keep it going but it was not necessary because everyone else bowed to the inevitable and started playing for the second place prize money.

Maurice Bembridge came close to a good round in the 1976

German Open at Bremen, the fine von Limburger course built through a mighty forest. Nearly every hole requires the golfer to do something fancy with the ball, bending it around the angles of the dog-legs, hitting it high or low and occasionally, even harder, hitting it straight. In the last round Bembridge's control was as complete as if he had a radio guidance system to manoeuvre the ball. Having safely put the title in the bag he wobbled a bit on the last two holes. By then it did not matter since he had collected six birdies and the loot by fully seven shots but he spoilt what had all the makings of a good round.

He had an even better chance the previous year in the Masters when he equalled the Augusta National record of 64, a feat which goes unremarked in the tournament's official history. Since we are talking about flawless rounds I have to deduct a point or two because he did overhit his tee shot at the short 12th and his ball finished in the back bunker.

He then played about the best sand shot I have ever seen. Had it been fractionally strong the ball would have picked up pace on the cruel slope and rolled on down to the pond. Had it been fractionally weak he would have left it in the bunker from his downhill lie. He flipped the ball to the edge of the green and the ball, fizzing with backspin, skidded slowly to the edge of the hole, rather like a tug o' war team digging in its heels as it is inexorably pulled over the line.

Jack Nicklaus is a great one for the occasional purple patch, although his unprecedented success as a tournament golfer is due more to the consistent avoidance of errors for round after round. Being a man of cautious disposition, it takes a real shock to blast his conservatism asunder and I count myself privileged to have been by the 13th green at Augusta when Nicklaus glanced up at the scoreboard and did a double-take. Snead was going mad and running away with the tournament. Everyone remembers that 1975 Masters for Johnny Miller's third round charge and his last round bid, along with Tom Weiskopf, to thwart Nicklaus's fifth title. But that victory was mounted on those early eight holes when Nicklaus took fright. He was at the height of his powers and, for once, going for the pin.

It was thrilling to watch and afterwards I put it to Nicklaus that he had only to continue in the same vein and win by 20 strokes and his rivals would be so intimidated that they would give him a walk-over for the Grand Slam. Nicklaus smiled wistfully and said that he could not bring himself to play like that unless he was stampeded into it. It is curious to reflect that inside the greatest professional of his era, or perhaps any other, there is an even greater player held prisoner by shackles of caution.

Both Miller and Weiskopf make my short list as contenders for a good round. Miller's charging 63 over a soggy Oakmont to win the 1973 US Open has rightly been acclaimed as one of the outstanding rounds in the history of the game, but I am not sure that it surpassed Weiskopf's disciplined last round to win the Open championship at Troon later that same year.

Tom Watson gets my prize for the best four consecutive rounds with his Open championship victory at Turnberry in 1977, followed by the closest possible margin by Nicklaus one stroke adrift in the same championship. Inevitably, Gary Player comes into the single round reckoning, particularly with nine birdies in the last round 64 which made up seven strokes on the leader and won him the 1978 Masters. That was almost a good round, blemished by the seventh hole where he hit his three-wood into the trees, recovered into a bunker, splashed out to five feet and then took two putts for a bogey. His 59 in Mexico sounds like a good round but, according to his playing companion, Priscillo Diniz, Player was all over the golf course. His recovery play was magnificent but for perfection of striking it did not approach Peter Alliss's 64 on the Old Course at St Andrews.

Two of the best part-rounds were Tony Jacklin's outward 29 at St Andrews and Jose-Maria Canizares' seven birdies and an eagle to be out in 27 in the Swiss Open. But these were purple patches only, the first to be thwarted by a cloudburst and the second by a rush of blood.

Eye witnesses rate Bernhard Langer's 62 in the last round to win the Spanish Open over the difficult El Saler Course, near Valencia, last year as a marvel, with 10 birdies and no dropped strokes, but alas I did not see it; pity, that, because it might have been a contender.

The nearest approach to a good round, with every shot going pretty well as intended, must be the opening 63 by Nicklaus at Baltusrol which set him up for a record total in each succeeding round of the 1980 US Open championship. Oddly enough, it was also there that I saw the best half-round of golf of my spectating career. The half in question was the portion from tee to green over 18 holes. The other half, the putting, was certainly the most pitiful I have witnessed, not excluding some of those early extravaganzas by Bernhard Langer. The competition was the 1967 US Open championship, won by Nicklaus, and the player, if you have not guessed already, was Ben Hogan.

The Observer, 1980

Golf according to Joe Public

He would not stand out in a crowd – a nondescript man, middle age, medium height, mid-brown hair. Airport delays make brothers of us all and we sat on adjacent bar stools, united by a common bond of frustration and hatred for the inconvenience of modern travel.

I was intrigued by the way he kept dipping a measuring stick into his Budweiser between sips. He noticed my interest.

'Three-point-seven fluid ounces and then I have to leave the rest.'

'If it is not too personal, may I enquire why?'

He groaned softly. 'I'm cursed. You know how in every country there is one hick town where they always vote the way the country votes? Well, that's me. I'm the average man of that average town. I'm so damned average it hurts. What I think, the nation thinks. What I do, the nation does. Or maybe it is the other way round. What's the difference?'

He handed me his card: JOE PUBLIC, 'The Man In The Street'.

'You see,' he said, 'the average American male adult consumes three-point-seven fluid ounces of beer a day so that is my ration. One more drop would kill me. You wouldn't believe how I get pestered by TV analysts, political pollsters and market researchers trying to find out what the nation thinks about things. What sort of plastic toy should they put in the cornflakes box? Will the public sit still for *Police Academy 9*? The other day I was asked what I thought about Japanese cars. I've got two Toyota wheels on my pick-up, that's the statistical norm of Japanese cars *per capita*, and I said they never gave me any trouble. Next day *Business Week* comes out with an article headed "America votes Japanese cars tops for reliability".'

'Do you play golf?' I asked.

'Of course. I am condemned to conform to all trends. I am supposed to play .252 holes a day but usually I save up a week's supply and play 1.764 holes on Saturday. Then I spend the evening at the club conforming to the national statistics on alcohol consumption. It isn't the amount, you understand, but the variety. I have to put away minute amounts of an incredible number of different types of muck. No wonder I can only manage point-five when I get home to the wife.'

'Point-five of what?'

'Love. American couples do it an average of 2.5 times a week. Would you like to see a picture of the wife? Here she is with the kids on our last vacation.'

'Very attractive. But whatever happened to the little chap?'

'Ah, that's Point Seven, poor kid. He is what comes of having to conform to the national average of 1.7 children per couple.'

'Yes, I can see there are serious disadvantages to being Joe Public. But on the other hand you have tremendous influence. What you say goes. For instance, you decide which golf competitions are accorded the status of major championships. How do you do that?'

'Take the Open Championship. Yes, I know that technically it is supposed to be called just the Open, but Joe Public calls it the British Open. Well, that makes it one because it was the first. Joe Public is very big on all that history and heritage stuff.

'I consider the Masters to be a major mainly because of Bobby Jones, but it has a lot more going for it, like the course, the continuity and the organisation.

'The PGA has gone down and they play it on some freaky tracks and pack the field with nobody club pros. But Joe Public is not fickle. The PGA used to be a proper major and it deserves to be a major, so I give it the benefit of the doubt in the hope that it will get its act together.

'The US Open is a major because it is the national championship of the premier golfing nation and the United States Golf Association goes to endless trouble to ensure that it is worthy of being called a major. It always chooses a great course and then prepares it in such a way that only a player with the temperament and technical skill of a true champion can possibly win it.'

'But what about those times when a thunderstorm floods the course and softens it so much than any run-of-the mill pro can handle it?' I asked. 'Do you call that a proper championship?'

'Heck no. Joe Public is not fooled by all that TV hyperbole. Flood a US Open course and you're left with just another Kemper Open.'

'So you are thinking of dropping the US Open as a major?'

'No, I would never do that. But I do think that just as soon as they have got the greens up to speed they should put covers on them at night. And, like they do in tennis, baseball and cricket, they should be ready to whip the covers onto the greens the minute the thunderstorm hooter is blown during play. That way the USGA can guarantee we have a true US Open every year and a true champion at the end of the week.'

Golf World, 1990

The sorcerer's golf course _____

On March 18, 1982, a major new championship will be born. In the years that follow, the new championship will grow in stature and, although it may never achieve the cachet of the venerable US and British Opens, it will acquire a special status as the ultimate test of a golfer's character and skill. This much is certain and beyond argument.

Now, if I may lapse into fanciful speculation for a moment, I foresee another development arising from the new major championship. The surplus cash raised by the tournament will be devoted to the endowment of a medical centre serving two specialized functions.

The clinic will have an intensive-care unit for the treatment of golf watchers who have toppled off the spectator mounds into the lake bordering the 18th fairway at the Players' Club course and have been attacked by alligators. It also will have a large wing of laboratories and padded rooms for care of professional golfers suffering from a previously unknown condition called Ponte Vedra Syndrome.

The symptoms of this tragic ailment will be an uncontrolled tendency by the patient to kick his caddie, to chew chunks out of the locker room carpet and to hide under the bed whimpering that somebody called Pete Dye is out to get him.

The new major event in question is, of course, the Tournament Players Championship, which next year moves to its new home, the Players' Club near Jacksonville. The course was designed by Pete Dye. I have never met him but I know him well and can describe him in the fullest detail. He is 500 years old and has absorbed the wisdom of the ages. He wears a pointed hat and flowing robe embroidered with occult symbols. When he speaks, he becomes extremely animated and gesticulates a lot, with flashes of blue static crackling from his long fingernails. If anyone has the temerity to suggest that possibly the contouring of a green is just a trifle severe, he whips out a cane, taps the wretch on the head and turns him into a frog.

A couple of years ago Commissioner Deane Beman sent for Dye and said: 'Behold this tract of jungle swamp. Pray turn it into the world's first golf stadium.' Dye gazed over the unpromising acres of marsh and impenetrable scrub. 'Certainly,' he said. 'Bring me a bulldozer and two quarts of Mountain Lion's Sweat, finest sipping whisky (not a drop is sold until it's two days old).'

'Drink this,' Dye commanded the bulldozer driver. The man did so and climbed unsteadily onto his machine. 'Now,' said Dye, 'cut a straight path through that lot.'

The machine lurched forward, weaving an erratic swath through the scrub. It looked like a natural track that had been there since the beginning of time, like the jungle paths trampled out by generations of elephants moving down to a watering hole.

For months Dye cast his spell over the landscape. He created a moat around the property to keep out the most dangerous predators of this modern age, the sabre-toothed property developers who, given half a chance, despoil golf courses with their hideous condominiums. At selected vantage points Dye created grassy terraces from which 40,000 spectators could observe the passing golfers going bananas.

Here and there he built recognizable golfing features, notably teeing grounds. At first sight I thought that tees were the only things he had built. There it was, a neatly mowed rectangle of turf with tee markers and a board with the usual legend: 'Hole one, 440 yards, par-four'. But he seemed to have neglected to provide the other normal appurtenances of golf, such as fairway and green.

Odd. I put on my distance glasses and peered across a wasteland of packed sand, lake and streams that snaked treacherously this way and that. Then I saw it, a glade of emerald grass about the size of a tennis court. It looked to be 300 yards away.

I pondered the problem. Suppose a player were to aim a drive to miss that tree by 2 inches, and suppose the ball then rose to fly the corner of that other tree, and suppose that hook spin then curved the flight of the ball on an oblique approach to pitch on that angled slope . . . Yes, theoretically it was possible for a true master of golf to land a ball on that patch of grass.

In my excitement I swung my driver and caught the ball a glancing blow off the toe, causing it to dart off at right angles and become jammed in the mesh of a trash basket.

Several strokes and two golf balls later I reached that patch of fairway and now the green was plainly visible – in a tiny clearing in the woods across a lake. All that was needed was a high, fading one-iron off my downsloping lie and, in principle, a ball might hold on that elephant's grave of a green.

I may not have recalled the precise distances and features of this opening hole, for you get punchy pretty quickly on the Players' Club course, but you get the idea.

Having got the field away to an easy start, Dye now begins to increase the severity of his masterpiece – or, as J. C. Snead describes it, a cross between a strip mine and *Star Wars*.

Every shot, from drive to the tap-in fourth putt, requires the golfer to recognize and solve a specific golfing problem before he attempts the stroke. Whereas most golf courses have 130 acres or so of maintained turf, this one has only 40 acres, sparingly allotted in islands of fairway and green. Water impinges on 16 of the holes, and totally surrounds the pocket-handkerchief green of the short 17th that is surely destined to become the most notorious short hole in America. I reckon it will invoke more blaspheming than the 16th at Cypress Point by a ratio of about two to one.

This is unashamedly a course for the experts. It is the most difficult course I have ever seen – and possibly the best. Club golfers will make pilgrimages to pit their puny skills against the monster, and they will not score within 10 strokes of their handicaps. If I were condemned to play for the rest of my life on one course, I would unhesitatingly choose this one and happily limit my ambitions to breaking 100.

From now on, for one week of every year, the world's finest golfers will be set to tackle this extreme examination of their talents. The TPC will be golf's equivalent of the Christians versus the lions. It may be sadism but it also will be sensational. I am willing to bet now that some illustrious player will lose his cool and fail to break 90. I hear disquieting rumours that certain faint-hearts are pressing for some of the greens to be modified. Get down there immediately, Mr Dye, and turn them into frogs.

Golf Digest, 1981

Europe's free market

It is not often that we innumerate yobs of the sports pages can teach the city slickers a thing or two but the ringing exhortations to British industry to prepare for the challenge of 1992 create a solemn duty to pass on the lessons of our experience.

Tournament golf, you see, experienced 1992 20 years ago. We have been through the tariff barrier into the free market jungle. And before anyone objects that sportsmen are very different from businessmen, let us wring the neck of that *petit canard* (note the fluent command of foreign languages after two decades of continental trading). Tournament golfers are all incorporated; they are all chairmen of the boards of small, export-based companies of the kind which will have to adapt to 1992 or die.

Looking through my diaries for 1972 and immediately beyond, I have to admit that the passage into the smooth waters of European growth and prosperity was pretty turbulent at times. The first lesson we learnt as an unofficial association of small businesses was to master the paperwork.

One employee who set off from Dublin to Switzerland, via Berlin, neglected to furnish himself with passport, visas or travel document-ation of any kind and it required considerable ingenuity on his part to elude the ticket collectors on sundry ferries and trains, not to mention immigration officials and the *volkspolizei* crossing East Germany. The sternest test of his cost-cutting business acumen arose when he had to continue his journey from Berlin to Switzer-land, which he accomplished by zipping himself into the travel cover of his boss's golf bag and having himself loaded onto the truck, or *camion* as you Euro-reps will have to learn to call it, which transported the scoreboard.

All went well until he unzipped the bag and appeared. The French driver, who understood not one word of the Wicklow dialect, turned off the autobahn in panic at this apparition, thoroughly lost his way and asked directions at an East German police station.

These days they are called lager louts but back in 1972 we simply called them Australians, and two such company chairmen used novel business methods at one Dutch Open. They were conferring with their associates when they were approached by two senior officials and politely reminded that caddies were not permitted in the clubhouse. Two right-handers brought the conference to an abrupt conclusion.

Another dispute, also in Holland, was resolved in the traditional pre-Thatcher British custom of a lightning strike. The senior shop steward shouted 'Down clubs, brothers' and the chairmen refused to play until some non-union Americans were dismissed. This impasse was resolved in a masterly compromise after hard negotiating with the management. Everyone played but the scab Americans com-peted in a separate but simultaneous competition for prize money donated by management.

Spain was a difficult territory in those days because the local small businessmen very properly saw the common market of golf as an opportunity for them, notably a Madrid taxi-driver who was engaged to take a chairman back to his hotel since he was weary after having been arrested twice during the course of an adventurous evening. When the taxi passed the same monument for the third time the chairman took swift executive action from the back seat, causing the vehicle to swerve violently. The chairman suffered his third arrest at the point of an automatic weapon and was unable to give a coherent account of the proceedings when questioned next day, beyond remarking: 'It didn't half make a mess of the shoe shop.'

On that same export drive another valuable lesson was learnt. About 20 chairmen discovered that their flight had been heavily over-booked and they were milling about in a mutinous mob when a Spanish-speaking chairman walked up to the check-in desk and produced a ticket of Varig Airlines. The clerk removed the flight coupon, which bore a strange resemblance to a high denomination banknote, and the late arrival was waved through to the departure lounge. When we arrived at the next tournament a day late and in ill-humour we discovered that he did not even have a booking, let alone a ticket, for that flight.

Italy was a tough market back in golf's 1992, giving us the best and worst experiences of the invisible export trade. In Sardinia, for instance, the airport coach eventually had to leave without two missing chairmen. As we drove along a narrow road through the dense shrubbery of the *macchia*, in which a kidnapper can remain undetected by a pursuing policeman passing within a yard or so, two bedraggled figures hailed the bus. They were caked in dust and blood, and neither was entirely coherent, one of them groaning 'Go like hell' as they collapsed on the back seat. By a democratic vote we decided that Bernhard Langer should station himself by the door as the toughest line of defence against boarders.

The incident of one chairman's successful sales pitch to three generations of the same tourist family, grandmother, mother and nubile daughter, during one night in Spain has gone into golfing lore but that was not strictly business so I shall not mention it.

Those pioneering days of opening up a free market back in 1992 may have been rough and tough but perseverance and a stash of bail money in the tournament director's briefcase eventually forged a true union of the nations and a mighty crock of gold. Of course it helped that golf is a gentleman's game, another lesson that British business could profitably ponder.

The Observer, 1989

If I were commissioner

Move over, Mr Beman. I have just been commanded to assume dictatorial powers over the PGA Tour for a day and to lay down policy guidelines that will transform professional golf into the most popular spectator sport in the country.

Golf ought to be able to surpass all rival sporting attractions, and it can if we go back to first principles and recognize sport's basic appeal as a substitute for war.

However, with its unbroken routine of 72-hole stroke events, professional golf has evolved into something closer to a substitute for an accountancy examination. It has become a game played with 14 clubs and a calculating machine (or abacus in the case of Lu Liang-huan).

Stroke play is the dullest form of golf and it gets progressively duller as standards rise. Perfect golf, if we can imagine such a thing, would not be worth watching. It can be argued that stroke-play golf of high standard became a major spectator sport, so the game must have a wide popular appeal. That is untrue. Arnold Palmer became a major spectator sport and the reason was because he played bad golf. He played bad golf better than anyone else, before or since.

Professionals do not like match play. They argue, fallaciously, that it is unfair for one man to survive, by beating an opponent with a 74 to a 75, while another player is eliminated after scoring a 68 to his opponent's 67. Even if we accept that dishonest expression of match play results in terms of medal scores, the charge of unfairness is still exposed as false. The player who survived after scoring 74 did what he had to do in his individual situation. Nobody can say that he would not have scored 66 if his opponent had pushed him to such limits.

So the first thing we do is give the tour a powerful injection of match-play golf and we cooperate with the networks in exploring TV techniques to present the high drama of head-to-head duelling.

The second thing we do is eliminate the money list, on the grounds that it is crass, inaccurate, historically misleading and has nothing whatsoever to do with sport, which is, remember, what we are promoting. (In 1945 Byron Nelson won 18 tournaments and finished with $63,335, which would have put him in 64th spot on last year's money list.)

Instead, we devise a simple player-rating system, based on tournament finishing positions. We might, for instance, allot 150 points for the player who enters a tournament and fails to prequalify.

The player who fails to make the cut will be given 100. Those playing the last two rounds get the figure for their final placing. These figures are averaged week by week, giving an accurate performance rating for every player at any moment in his career and providing valid comparisons with every golfer in the history of the game.*

Now, having reasserted golf as a sport, we take advantage of the biggest single factor in the popularity of sporting contests. Why do those tedious games such as basketball, football and baseball command such massive public support? Because they engage the powerful emotion of local loyalty. The people of Los Angeles follow the Rams through thick and thin because this is their team.

So my third decree is that every golfer upon receiving his card must nominate his state or national affiliation, according to his choice and on the basis of his birthplace, his university or his home. Golf is now able to involve local passions. We might have an interstate foursomes knockout competition, possibly a mixed foursomes with the cooperation of the LPGA. Even in our bread-and-butter stroke-play tournaments we could pursue the state championships. Players not directly in contention would still provoke high interest because the player seeking to finish 65th instead of 66th might well be fighting for the vital point by which Texas beats Florida.

These are not gimmicks. Match play, foursomes, team play and mixed foursomes are all traditional and honourable forms of the game and professional golfers ought to add them to their repertory. It would be good for them and good for golf. Mix up the diet of the tour and you would have to beat off the spectators with a stick.

Since my term of office lasts only one day, I must leave the detailed planning to Mr Beman and his staff. He and they have done a terrific job of building the tour and preserving the integrity of golf. All I am really suggesting is that the tour add the spice of vision and imagination to its well-proven recipe.

Golf Digest, 1981

---

*The Sony World Rankings, which were introduced some years later, employ this system in somewhat more sophisticated detail.

Quote me a quote

Once upon a time before you and I were born it was the custom of newspapers to carry reports of sporting events. Our correspondent would go along to, say, a cricket match and describe what he saw. 'Grace dispatched the crimson orb to the confines for the full complement.' And much, much more in similar captivating style.

These days readers are not interested in what a player did. They are fascinated to learn what a player said he did. Unless a sportsman can talk a good game he is nothing. I am old enough to remember when the craze of quote-journalism first fired the imagination of sports editors and, as a practitioner in the field, it was uphill work, I can tell you.

At a tournament in Yorkshire Neil Coles and Bernard Hunt were playing together. Of course, being professionals, they were never favoured with the use of their Christian names, thereby becoming the source of frequent nightmares for the late Henry Longhurst, the pioneer TV commentator.

Coles and Hunt were professionals of the old school, brought up in the tradition that sportsmen should be seen and not heard. They simply could not take to this new-fangled idea of answering questions and in those early interviews they responded mostly with embarrassed grunts. On this occasion they had both scored well and were duly wheeled into the press tent to be grilled for the day's quotes. Hunt first. 'Drive, six, two putts. Drive, edge, two putts. . . .' The recital continued to the 14th hole. 'Drive, four, two putts.' At this point Coles, who was just beginning to grasp the fundamentals of the new journalism, gave a faint cough and raised one eyebrow about a millimetre. Hunt stopped his recital and looked at Coles in bewilderment.

'Aren't you going to tell them about the 14th?' whispered Coles. 'The 14th?' said Hunt. 'Regulation par.' 'No,' hissed Coles. 'You know . . .' Say what you like about us sports writers but we can sniff a story. 'What happened at the 14th?' we bayed. It was like drawing teeth but we persisted and bit by bit it all came out. As he was addressing the ball for the approach shot Hunt's club was struck from his hands by lightning.

Eventually we had our story, justifying the new system for it was almost as good as if we had seen the incident ourselves, although try as we might we couldn't get much of a quote out of Hunt. What did you do when lightning hit you? 'I picked up the club and hit the ball.

Front left, about twenty feet.' Not the most arresting utterance you have heard, perhaps, but it was a start.

How times have changed. Ten years later the players had mastered the art of the quote. When Lee Trevino was hit by lightning at the Western Open he did 30 minutes of stand-up comedy patter without drawing breath and he had a column of quotes in every newspaper. That is why he is a superstar.

These days young professionals are taught the art of the quote at the American qualifying school and they have to sign a declaration agreeing to cooperate with the media at all times, meaning that they must be ready with a quotable quote at the drop of a tape recorder.

The most important time for quotes is before a tournament when the newspapers are obsessively devoting columns and columns to reports of what is going to happen. This is one of my favourite journalistic exercises and I live for the day when I master the art of prognostication to such a degree that it will not be necessary to report the actual event at all. I shall simply write: 'The Open championship was played yesterday and turned out exactly as I forecast five days ago. Back numbers are available from the circulation department.'

Arnold Palmer is the absolute master of the quote and I cherish particularly his reply to a quote-hungry writer before the US Open championship. 'Do you think the guys can shoot low on this course, Arnie?' 'Waaall, any time you drive the ball in the fairway, hit all the greens and make a bunch of putts then you have a chance to make a good score.'

When professionals are talking about their own play their remarks can only be properly understood if you happen to know their scores. I have therefore invented a new form of punctuation which I hope will be universally adopted by newspapers for golfing quotes. Here is how it works.

Jerry Pate led the first round and said: 63 I really enjoyed playing this superb course which has been beautifully prepared for the championship. 63

Or. Larry Nelson commented: 75 They could do with lowering the cutters of the fairway mowers; I had a lot of flyers. 75

Or. Lanny Wadkins snarled: 82 I'd like to get hold of the clown who set those pin positions and give him a lobotomy – with my wedge. 82

By now we experienced hands, both players and writers, have refined the quotes business to a fine art. I glance at the scoreboard and notice that David Graham, for instance, has been posted with a score of 76. A few years ago this would have required a complicated ritual involving a tape recorder and laborious transcription, followed by the editing out of any fruity adjectives and then the writing of the rough draft. Now, under the mutual trust system, the process can be streamlined.

Self: 'How?'

Graham: 'Tripled five.'

I can now go straight to the typewriter and begin: 'David Graham's challenge faltered with a third round 76. An otherwise solid performance was marred by a torrid seven at the innocuous 370-yard fifth hole where the players enjoyed the help of a light following breeze. Graham reeled from the course ashen faced and groaned: 'I played that hole like an arthritic granny.'

You may purse your lips and mutter about a decline in journalistic ethics but it is necessary to invent quotes more and more these days because professional golfers are gradually losing the power of speech. Already adverbs have been eliminated entirely from their vocabulary. 'I hit the ball super but putted just horrible.' Some of these semantic murderers have gone further and limit themselves to the use of one adjective only, employing it on every possible occasion and sometimes in the middle of a word, thus: 'I played a low com-****-pression ball.'

These developments in the world of golf reporting have transformed our lives. We cannot waste time enjoying the sunshine and fresh air on the golf course because hard necessity requires us to produce quotes. For reasons which I have explained we mostly have to invent such quotes, putting a gigantic strain on the imagination. The only way this can be achieved successfully, day after day, is by the use of artificial stimulants. Greatly against my natural inclinations, and indeed to my abhorrence, I myself have occasionally to resort to the use of hallucinatory drugs, of which alcohol is the only form available in golf clubs. So if you should happen to see a golf writer in the bar while a tournament is in progress, please suppress that unfortunately common instinct to remark sneeringly: 'I thought you reporter chappies were paid to watch golf.'

We are sensitive to such ignorant jibes. Just remember that as we force ourselves to swallow that hateful amber fluid through clenched teeth we are actually performing a difficult and distasteful task for *your benefit* and in order to support our families.

Golf World, 1979

Opening up the Open

Prominent among the tribal superstitions of American professional golfers is the notion that the Open championship, or British Open as they call it, is old-fashioned and unbearably pretentious. This notion is based in part on received wisdom that has been handed down through successive generations, such as Sam Snead's declaration that any time you go to Britain, you are camping out. Sam was a callow youth in those days, which roughly dates his remark in the era when we natives were just abandoning the practice of painting our bodies with woad. In part the legend derives from the fact that the Open, which is being played this week at Royal Birkdale in Southport, actually *is* old-fashioned and unbearably pretentious.

Even so, it is unchallenged as a golf tournament. It is not my purpose to argue that the Open is the greatest of the four championships by which we measure the stature of the world's finest players. Comparisons are said to be odious and, while I would never shrink from stooping to odium, simple facts are sufficient to demonstrate my point that the Open is the only major championship which is completely open to all the world and therefore valued as a truly international contest.

The PGA championship is simply an American tour event with ideas above its station. The United States Open is technically open to the world, but the qualifying process is so protracted that for practical purposes it is limited to American residents and a token Spaniard. As for the Masters, it is unashamedly an invitation event. The Swiss professional Gerald Hoppy could never have an opportunity to display his skills at Augusta, in contrast to the open-door policy of the Open.

You have never heard of Gerald Hoppy, and for good reason, but before we come to him, I must first introduce his golfing antecedents in order to demonstrate that in British golf, at least, the word 'open' is not used as a loose synonym for 'closed'.

In 1965, a Milwaukee postal sorter named Walter Danecki became frustrated by the American PGA's adamant refusal to accept his membership because of the narrow-minded technicality that he could not hit his hat. Accordingly, he unilaterally declared himself a professional and submitted his entry for the Open championship. In the qualifying competition, he returned scores of 108 and 113 and then expressed his appreciation of the small ball, saying that if he had been forced to play the larger-sized American ball he would have been all over the place. When asked why he had undertaken such a rash enterprise, he replied with disarming candour: 'I wanted the pot of gold.' The Royal and Ancient Golf Club of St Andrews soon afterwards made the big ball compulsory for the Open; sadly, Walter has never been back.

However, in 1976 a crane driver from Barrow-in-Furness, one Maurice Flitcroft, entered for the Open as an unattached professional despite the fact that his only golfing experience had been to hit a few chip shots on the beach. His first 18 holes of golf was therefore the first qualifying round at Hillside, near Liverpool, and, while his bemused marker was not totally confident that he had recorded every stroke of Maurice's wild hacking and flailing, he was prepared to sign the card for 121. Officials suggested with some vigour that Maurice need not put himself to the trouble of continuing.

You may point out that, in banishing Maurice from the course, the Royal and Ancient was betraying the very policy of free and open competition that I am seeking to defend. If so, you seriously misjudge the resourcefulness of Maurice Flitcroft, which brings me back to Gerald Hoppy.

Gerald Hoppy is a figment of Maurice's imagination, as was the red herring of his Swiss residence. By 1983, the Open had grown to such an extent that regional qualifying rounds had been introduced to winnow the flimsiest chaff from the wheat. Accordingly, Gerald Hoppy, actually Maurice Flitcroft, presented himself at Pleasington Golf Club, near Blackburn, last Monday to take the first faltering steps to fame and fortune.

An astute observer of the game might well have quickly penetrated the assumed name and disguised appearance of our hero because there was something unmistakably Flitcroftian about the way he needed five frenzied putts to hole out from 8 feet on the first green. But it was not until the turn, by which time he had expended 63 strokes, that the heavy hand of officialdom descended on Maurice's neck and he was again given the Royal and Ancient's version of the bum's rush.

All this makes my case that the Open is the only golf championship which conforms to the first principle of the sport, namely that everyone should have an equal opportunity.

Lee Trevino, who won the Open at Birkdale, expressed the view that it was the most American of the British championship courses, an opinion presumably based on the fact that there is a McDonald's hamburger palace in Southport. The course resembles the television pictures sent back from the moon, which explains why the British have shown no inclination to institute a space programme when lunar landscapes are within easy reach of the railway system.

The sheer strangeness of the championship links is itself of immense benefit to the golf. After all, the game is supposed to be much more than a test of straight hitting. At Birkdale, the players will encounter terrain and vegetation and golfing dilemmas such as they have never met before. All their powers of resourcefulness, stoicism, patience and survival will be examined to the limit – and that in just trying to get a cup of coffee through room service.

The champion golfer, as the winner is designated for a year, will not only be a hell of a golfer but he will also be a hell of a man. If it is any consolation, on postwar experience he will almost certainly be an American, or the token Spaniard. Honour him well, whomever he may be, for he is the only genuine champion of golf.

The Guardian, 1983

Golfers on a short fuse ──────────

So far as we know golf grew to popularity on the east coast of Scotland round about the year 1430 and so it is safe to assume that by 1450 people were going round shaking their heads in a nostalgic manner and complaining: 'There aren't any characters in the game any more.' Certainly by the end of the century the phrase was well established in the litany of golf, along with 'Never up, never in' and 'Golf is a humbling game.'

It was not true then and it is not true now and it will never be true so long as the human character is spiced with the ingredient called temper. Younger readers may be unfamiliar with the monologues of Marriott Edgar, and it is their loss, but that wonderful Lancashire music hall performer wrote an ode which exactly traces the emotional sequence of my favourite golf incident. The poem starts:

'Joe Ramsbottom rented a bit of a farm
From its owner, Squire Goslett his name;

And the Gosletts came over with William the First,
And found Ramsbottoms here when they came.'

The event described in this ditty was that Joe broke the coulter on
his plough, decided that it would save time if he borrowed a spare one
from the nearby Squire's farm, felt that such a request might be
presumptuous, berated himself for his diffidence since it was the
Squire's rock which had busted his plough, assured himself that he
was as good as any stuck-up Squire and, having received a friendly
greeting at the front door, let fly with the final verse:

'Then he said "P'raps you think yourself better than me
Well, I'm telling you straight that you're not,
And I don't want your coulter, your plough or your farm,
You can—do what you like with the lot." '

Clayton Heafner was a pretty fair golfer and a spiritual brother
of Joe Ramsbottom. Driving to one tournament Clayton began to
reflect on his last visit to this club and how he had had to climb a
tree to dislodge his ball, no paltry feat for a man of his bulk. This
and sundry other memories mingled with the yeast of his temper
and by the time he drove into the club's car park the fermentation
was bubbling dangerously. He stopped the car, yelled 'You can
keep your goddam trees and your whole goddam golf course' and
drove off again.

Another American of that pre-war era, Lefty Stackhouse, was
also a slow boiler. He made valiant efforts to keep himself in
control and might finish his round with complete decorum but
experienced Stackhouse watchers knew that there was a formidable head of pressure within his powerful frame and waited for the
delayed reaction. Suddenly he would explode, breaking all his
clubs or, on one occasion, systematically demolishing his roadster
in the car park. On balance it was probably preferable when he got
it out of his system there and then, which he did by punching
himself on the jaw or kicking himself in the leg. Lefty was a pretty
keen and pretty regular performer with the bottle and one day, in
his woozy condition, he laid himself out cold on the golf course with
a right hook.

The commonest form of golfing outrage takes the form of
uncontrolled hatred for the equipment of the game, mostly the
putter. In his youth our own Mark James, today a golfer of
impeccable deportment, went through a phase of marked anti-
pathy towards his feckless putter. Their relationship deteriorated
to such a degree during the Bob Hope Benefit Classic, or whatever
it was called, at the RAC country club, Epsom, that he kicked the

club all round the car park and then threw it into a bush, saying: 'You can stay there all night and we'll see if that teaches you how to behave.'

Ky Laffoon, who is almost invariably and erroneously referred to as part Red Indian, used to tie his putter to a string and tow it behind his car as he travelled from tournament to tournament to punish it for its sins. The club suffered severe damage as it crashed and bounced on the roadway and Laffoon used to repair it by pressing it hard onto the road surface as he sped along, grinding off the bumps and sending up a shower of sparks.

Eddie Polland had the shortest of fuses when he first became a tournament professional. It was almost a double swing. Slow back. Accelerate down. Ball in rough. Accelerate back again. Even faster acceleration down into tee box. Crash. Splinter. He carried his clubs in a shoulder bag in those days and it looked as if it had been mauled by a tiger. There were cuts everywhere, caused by assaults with his irons, and distinct tooth impressions from his attempts to bite out the heart of his enemy. Then one day Eddie took stock of himself and decided that he would never get anywhere in golf if he allowed his emotions to get the better of him. He made an instant and complete conversion. From that day onwards he took everything in his stride, grinning at the worst indignities that fate could throw at him and never responding with so much as a 'Tut, tut.'

Ken Brown does not abuse his clubs. He does not curse. He does not kick locker doors off their hinges. He does not lose his head. But he suffers the agonies of the damned and he directs his outrage inwardly, at himself. He has an innocent, over-simplified view of golf which is that if he does his job properly then his drives will finish in the centre of the fairways and his approach shots will go into the hole. If perchance some unkindly bounce should prevent his approach shot from finding the cup then he will put the ball away with one stroke of his trusty putter. That is his job and purpose in life. Nothing less will satisfy him and the winning of a tournament is no kind of consolation if he has failed in his high endeavour.

Thus when he won the Glasgow Classic by 11 strokes this year he could not contain his disappointment. The shame of failure was insupportable and he could not trust himself to speak. Choking back his sobs of self-reproof he hurled his clubs into the boot of his car and drove off furiously into the night.

It would not be true to say that Tommy Bolt had the worst temper in golf because we all know some veritable volcanoes in the amateur game, including one of my acquaintance who emits a horrible curse of disappointment as he takes the putter back. But Bolt is the most famous exponent of the popping cork and even writes instructional articles on the art, advocating such policies as making sure that you throw the club forward. Saves the legs.

Apart from throwing and breaking clubs, Bolt also had a lurid vocabulary and his expletives sometimes reached the ears of the gallery. That would never do and the American PGA instituted a system of fines to curb his tongue, 100 dollars per cuss word. A monitor was appointed to follow Bolt around the course and keep tally of his language. At the end of the round the committee sent for Bolt and fined him 200 dollars. He paid up and went to the bar, where his fellow pros were surprised to see him sipping his drink and smiling like a cat which had swallowed the canary. Since his demeanour suggested that it was safe to approach him, a player observed that he looked remarkably cheerful considering that they had just fined him 200 dollars. 'Yes,' said Bolt smugly, 'but I stiffed the bastards for 1,500 bucks.'

The Observer, 1984

Chapter 3

Art or science? Just hit it

Faders don't fade away

Oh, very well then. You have been extremely patient. For something like 500 years you have been waiting to learn the secret of golf and finally I have decided to reveal it. As a matter of fact, it has been revealed before. Harry Vardon spelled it out. So did Bobby Jones. Ben Hogan realized it late in his career and told the world. Nobody listened because there was no way to prove that the secret worked.

Now that the US tour is keeping full statistics, and people are paying attention to them, the secret of golf is uncovered for all to see. All you have to do is aim your drive down the left side of the fairway and hit with a high fade.

Why, oh why, you ask, have I waited so long to divulge this information ? Well, it all goes back to those far-off days when aeroplanes had propellers and a foolhardy US Navy undertook to teach me to fly. Hatchet-faced instructors would assess the progress of us intrepid birdmen and grade us in terms of baseball statistics. Knowing nothing of baseball, and less of baseball statistics, I never knew how I was doing.

But anyway, we won the war and I emerged as a staunch disciple of Winston Churchill's dictum that there are lies, damned lies and statistics. Particularly sports statistics.

This lifelong mistrust of sporting statistics drew me naturally to golf, a game blessedly free of decimal points and performance averages. Until last year. Then the US tour started measuring and analysing the game, and in the line of duty I have spent four months with a cold towel wrapped around my spinning head, trying to make sense out of the statistics.

The first thing to do is reject the obviously idiotic figures. The money list, for example, is meaningless since it makes no distinction between the golfer who played 40 tournaments and the player who teed it up only 12 times. Instead, we must look to the stroke averages for a measure of performance. Likewise, we can dismiss the tables for birdies and eagles, since these simply reflect a summary of golfing skills. And while we are about it, we can toss those putting statistics into the trash basket because they are hopelessly biased in favour of the player who misses greens, chips up to the flag and holes out from 18 inches. They tell us nothing about putting skill as such.

The revealing tour statistics are those for driving distance, driving accuracy, hitting greens in regulation, sand saves and scoring averages. First, this exciting business of giving the ball a big bash off the tee. Driving distance is revealed as golf's major false god. Anyone who averages 260 yards off the tee must be rated a long hitter but those who strive for an extra 10 yards are simply slugging themselves into oblivion.

Driving accuracy (given a decent quantity of horsepower in the shot) is much, much more important than distance. Jack Nicklaus is the only player who drives the ball both long and straight and his rank in accuracy off the tee (13th) is somewhat falsified by his tactics of occasionally deliberately firing his ball into light rough for position. It may sound trite, but the art of good golf as shown by the statistics is to put your shot into position from where you can hit the green in regulation figures.

That conclusion, which can now be backed by statistical proof, leads me to the all-important secret of golf. From personal observation I would say that nine pro golfers out of 10 draw their drives, as the result of an obsession for length. They start as kids, striving for every inch of length because of their simplistic reasoning that the shorter the second shot the lower the score. They won't be told. Explain that a faded drive down the left makes the fairway twice as wide and they reverse the argument, saying that a hooked drive down the right has the same effect. It doesn't. The high faded ball sits where it lands while the hooked ball pitches and runs – into trouble as likely as not. That is the real story of the tour statistics.

Are you still unconvinced? Then I invite you to run your eye down the scoring averages and, if you must, down the money list. In both cases the top-10 leaders of 1980 are players who fade the ball. The one incongruity is Andy Bean, whose natural shot is right to left. Three years ago I daresay that Bean would have been the leader in driving distance, for he used to give the ball an almighty smash and hook it back into the fairway. Today he is only just in the top 30 for distance off the tee for he has seen the light. He is a reformed hooker and that is vastly encouraging.

I believe it was Arnold Palmer who remarked that all pros are fighting a hook. In his case it was certainly true, but he never got the club into a position at the top to make a sweet pass at the ball and he had to turn himself inside out on the downswing to avoid a real snapper.

So there's the secret: fight that hook, and if the ball still goes left, then fight harder – until you have mastered that lovely, money-winning high fade.

Golf World, 1980

Prepare for the worst

The worst sin of handicap golfers, and I would say that this applies to 90 per cent of people who play for fun, is to underclub on approach shots. Now most of us play casual, friendly matches and on these occasions, when there is no precious medal at stake, there are certain variations that can be introduced into the game to add a certain novelty and help improve our tactical ideas.

As a young man, Henry Cotton and his friends had a rule that if anyone was playing for the flag, be it with a full wood or iron shot, pitch, chip or putt, and the ball finished short of the hole he had to pay the others sixpence.

Another variation, which can be used in conjunction with the previous rule if you like, is that every time you leave a putt short you have to move the ball a club-length farther away from the hole before you play your next putt.

The majority of professionals try in their practice rounds, which are the equivalent of the amateur sociable four-ball, to reproduce the tensions of the coming tournament. They play companionable but fierce money matches, which, with automatic press bets and individual matches, as well as partnership matches, can amount to a sizable chunk of cash. A few tournament players, too few in my opinion, treat the practice round as an expedition of exploration and set out to learn as much about the course as possible, especially the potential dangers.

Peter Thomson is the best example in my experience, although Jack Nicklaus is exceptionally thorough in a different way. To watch Thomson you would think he was a terrible player and you would have a hard time believing that he had won five British Open championships. No wonder nobody will play with him, you might tell yourself, as you see him drive into the rough and hit one approach after another into the bunkers.

At the end of the day, however, he knows exactly which are the problem areas of the course, which bunkers to respect, how the ball will behave when hit from different types of rough and which are the safest lines to the greens. His approach play in practice looks sloppy because, unless he is in a bunker, he tries to hit to a corner of the green well away from the hole.

The reason for this, as you may now suspect, is because he is shrewdly anticipating where the holes will be cut when the championship starts. You and I, if I may presume to assume that we share the same human frailties, hope and expect that the drive will go plumb centre to set up a perfect approach shot. Thomson knows that golf is hardly ever like that. The odd shot will stray and when it does he is ready for it, because he has already experienced that trouble shot and knows how to handle it.

Seve Ballesteros is the supreme example of a golfer whose morale does not wobble when he gets into difficulties. Nobody is better at getting out of trouble because nobody has practised harder on recovery shots. My strongest memories of him over the years are not of his famous victories but of his behaviour after finishing his round at tournaments. He would be out with his wedge and a few friends, stamping the ball into the turf, or throwing it into deep rough, or burying it in sand and betting on his chances of getting it close to the hole.

There we have the paradox of golf. We bad players cling to the fatuous belief that everything is going to go well, and conduct our golfing lives on that absurd premise, while the really good players know all too well that with this game things are bound to go horribly wrong, and they make provisions for these inevitable disasters.

Golf World, 1978

Wanted: a new Messiah

Opinions in golf go in fashions. Do you remember the late-hit craze? Somebody, probably Ben Hogan although I am open to correction, said that the late hit was what separated the pros from the amateurs. Millions of golfers tried to master the secret of the late hit without knowing what it meant or, to be precise, without realising that the expression was meaningless. The whole thing blew up into prominence because cameras of the day distorted the mechanics of the swing and then a new craze came along and everybody forgot about trying to hit late.

Then there was the business of 'drive for show and putt for dough'. That had a ring to it and seemed, like 'Never up, never in', to encapsulate an essential truth. It took some of us years to shake those gems of wisdom from our minds and see them for what they were, trite to the point of banality. Willie Park's famous battle cry: 'The man who can putt is a match for anyone', is another example of golfing booby-talk which had a considerable vogue.

Now I believe we are in for another glib and questionable generalisation. These days tournament golfers are subjected to the compulsory interview after any round lower than 72. Being taken into the pressroom has become a ritual and a small reward, less than a medal but a commendation in the form of a warm beer and a mention in the papers. The ritual aspect of the interview involves a shot-by-shot recital of the round. The old hands get through their litany at high speed, like a vicar at a thinly congregated Evensong when there is steak for dinner. 'First: drive, four-iron, two putts. Second: five-iron, 20-footer. . . .'

The novices stumble and forget their clubbing and the holes.

'What's that par-five on the front?' Well-organised writers who have furnished themselves with a card of the course supply the hole number. 'Well, I came off my tee shot and wound up in the right rough.' 'What club?' 'Driver – no, I took my three-wood.'

Being dutiful servants of our readers, we take copious notes. Besides, it would be impolite to just sit there yawning. (As soon as the player has left the room we throw away these notes on the grounds that they make duller reading than the London telephone directory.) What we want is electrifying copy, preferably involving stark human drama, incredible hardships, violence, hard drugs, big money or sex, preferably all of them. Since professional golfers are mainly level-headed, clean-living young men we are mostly disappointed, but we keep probing for a quotable quote. What we are getting more and more these days is the opinion that the day of the superstar is over. 'The depth of the tour is now so strong that anybody can win any week. Not so long ago there were perhaps 10 or 20 players in the field who were capable of winning but nowadays every guy who makes the cut is a potential winner.'

Goodness knows who started this notion. I suspect that it was a line dreamed up by a backroom publicist of the American tour to promote the idea that golf has produced a race of supermen of uniform excellence and to blur the fact that Jack Nicklaus, Arnold Palmer and Gary Player are getting a bit long in the tooth and can no longer do the business week after week.

Sophistry is dangerous stuff because it is essentially plausible. It is self-evident that any professional can win any tournament in theory. Further, you can back up that claim with 'proof' by listing some recent unlikely tournament winners, provided you omit the relevant fact that the tournaments in question did not attract the presence of the full complement of established stars. You might as well argue that because I have a typewriter and a supply of paper there is nothing to stop me from walking away with the Nobel prize for literature. Keep about a million good writers out of the contest and I might stand a chance.

The day of the superstar, I am convinced, is far from over. Lee Trevino recently gave a frank appraisal of his contemporary superstars in support of his theme that all of them had weaknesses. Nicklaus lacked a short game; Severiano Ballesteros was inconsistent with the driver; Bill Rogers was so slightly built that he did not have the strength and stamina for sustained golf; Tom Watson had only one speed, full ahead. He could not play a soft shot. Gary Player suffered from a hook. As for himself, Trevino was handicapped by a lack of length. 'The Lord,' he said, 'does not give anyone everything. He always holds back something.'

Nobody would quarrel with Trevino's assessments, but I suspect that his conclusion that every person is flawed by divine intention will be challenged by theologians and golfers alike. Why on earth or, indeed, in heaven should there not be a golfer who has everything? Bobby Jones came close to being the ideal all-round golfer with no obvious weaknesses. Byron Nelson tamed the game of golf, briefly but gloriously. Henry Cotton, Ben Hogan and Harry Vardon had just about everything except for consistent putting strokes.

As for that bleak appraisal that the day of the superstar is past for ever, I reject it totally. There will be new superstars and the odds are that one of them will surpass anything we have yet seen in golf. I just hope that I am around to watch him.

The Observer, 1982

The received balderdash of putting

Dear Mark James,

You will recall our conversation about putting on the practice green during the German Open. It therefore distressed me greatly that your putting average did not immediately drop to 27.5 and that in your next tournament, the Carrolls Irish Open, you qualified dead last. You clearly need help on the greens and so I have been canvassing hints on your behalf from the finest putters this game has ever known. For days I have been reading instructional books and studying action photographs and now I am able to pass on the accumulated wisdom of the masters of putting.

First the putter itself. Are you sure that you have the right type of club? Everyone says that this is vital. **Abe Mitchell** and **James Braid** assert that an aluminium headed putter is much to be preferred to the cleek (or blade putter, as we now know it). **Willie Park**, the putting genius of his day, puts it another way: you must use a cleek putter.

Now the grip. You hold the club in a two-handed grip with the right forefinger, the 'over forties' finger', down the shaft. Come, come. Watch **Orville Moody**, with his left hand below the right. Or **Phil Rodgers**, jamming the club into his belly button with the left hand and placing his right hand well below the grip on the bare shaft. Better still, listen to all the great putters of the modern era – **Jack Nicklaus, Arnold Palmer, Billy Casper, Ben Crenshaw** – and settle for a reverse overlap. **Bobby Locke**, the greatest of them all, said: 'The reverse overlap did nothing for my putting and it had an adverse effect on the rest of my game.'

With that settled, we can move on to the ticklish matter of how tightly to grip the club. 'Loosely' says Locke and Sam Snead advises that if you have problems with the shorties then grip tightly.

We are ready to take the stance which should be wide open (**Arnaud Massy**), square (Palmer) or closed (Casper). There is much the same consensus on how far apart the feet should be spread: like the front legs of a grazing giraffe (**Hubert Green**) or medium (Palmer) or together (Locke). Keep your weight predominantly on the left foot (**Lee Trevino**) and on the right foot (Massy) and have the ball positioned opposite the right toe (Park: 'It is easier to pull the ball into the hole with the left hand') and opposite the left toe (**Johnny Miller**: 'It is an underhand movement of the right hand.' Green: 'The bottom hand is in control.'). At the address the hands should be ahead of the ball (Green) and slightly behind the ball (Nicklaus).

All clear so far? The position of the head is vital, as all the experts agree – slap bang above the ball or, in the words of Nicklaus, behind it. You won't need me to tell you how important it is to keep the body as still as a rock during the stroke; that is quite obvious from the way that **Bob Murphy** sways about a yard and almost topples off balance. 'There should be no attempt to hold the body immovable' – **Bobby Jones**.

Tension is the enemy of putting and you will no doubt be familiar

with the old dodge of breathing out just before you begin the stroke. **Tommy Bolt** put it succinctly: 'Take a deep breath before you start your stroke.'

There is absolutely no conflict among the great putters about the type of stroke to be played, which should be a firm rap (Casper) or, in the words of **Sandy Herd**: 'You should coax the ball into the hole.' In order to achieve overspin, highly desirable stuff as all agree and meaning that the ball should roll towards the hole and not away from it, the ball should be hit slightly on the upswing (**Harry Weetman**) with a slightly descending blow (**George Duncan**).

Whatever you do, don't try to hit up on the ball to give it overspin (**Ben Hogan**) and eliminate all suspicion of wrist work to give the ball overspin (**Locke**).

So much for the essentials of technique, which you can practise and perfect, but I am conscious that nothing so far has described for you the feeling which must accompany your smooth, flowing, sharp rap. I think it is best summed up by **Tony Lema** and **Ted Ray** who said, respectively: 'The wrists are hinges and the club is swung like a pendulum' and: 'The one argument I cannot agree with is that the putter should be held much in the manner of a pendulum.'

You will forgive me for mentioning anything quite so obvious and fundamental but you are not by any chance doubtful about the angle of the blade at impact, are you? I know that it is the obvious which gets overlooked. As the club-head comes into the ball the face should be absolutely square to the target line (Casper) and slightly closed or hooded (Duncan) and just fractionally open (**Jack White**).

That's really all there is to putting, except to remember the dictum of Jack Nicklaus who said that putting was 2 per cent technique and 98 per cent inspiration or confidence or touch or luck.

Actually, if you have absorbed all this good advice you won't need luck.

The Observer, 1981

Keep it simple

A reader writes in a state of some alarm and dismay in response to my report that Jack Nicklaus now considers his book *Golf My Way* to be obsolete.

Nicklaus made this remark as an afterthought to his explanation of why he has found a new enthusiasm for the game. In recent years he has been practising his profession with the sole objective of adding to his tally of major championships, leaving him pretty much uninterested in bread and butter tournaments.

Now, however, he has resumed the learning process. His faithful tutor, Jack Grout, has been working with him on his swing and Phil Rodgers, the portly genius of the short game, has been initiating him into the secrets of pitching, chipping and sand play.

As a result, Nicklaus believes that his game is not even close to his standards of 10 years ago when he wrote the book. However, when Nicklaus says that he is twice the golfer he was when he wrote the book, he is talking about extremely advanced and esoteric areas of the game with which we need not concern the club player.

Harry, Don and Doug, who tell me that they live by *Golf My Way* and feel lost and abandoned now that the Master has declared his faith in new truths about the game, need not despair.

The basic tenets of golf, which Nicklaus outlined and which are as much as most of us can ever hope to master, remain unchanged. The 'body and legs' method of achieving power is as valid as ever, for those to whom it is suitable, and so is the famous 'flying right elbow'.

Incidentally, on the subject of the flying right elbow, I attended an instructive and vastly amusing clinic given by the great Bob Toski, who has assumed the mantle of Ernest Jones as the high priest of the Swing-the-club school of golf instruction. (Which is how you should seek to play if you are a natural swinger, as opposed to a natural body and legs hitter.)

Toski clamped his right elbow to his right hip and invited a challenge from anyone in the audience to a ball throwing contest if the challenger would keep his elbow in this position, merely flicking the ball with hand and wrist action. That demonstration made the point well, for in throwing a ball you have to let the elbow move clear of the body although, having taken the hand back, the first instinctive action is to pull the elbow towards the hip. If you attempt to keep that right elbow clamped to your side throughout the swing you are doomed.

Back to Nicklaus. At the start of his take-away he has always shown a tendency to tilt the shoulders and one of the improvements he has been striving to effect is to adjust the set of his shoulders at the address and then turn, right from the moment the club-head pulls back from the ball. Brian Barnes is another great player with this idiosyncrasy and he too has been working to change his tilt into a turn.

The effect of the change is to keep the path of the club-head in the correct plane on the upswing. What, you may ask, is the difference so long as you arrive at a good position at the top? After all, that is where the swing starts from. No. The swing is a reciprocating action and the rhythm and accuracy of the downswing is established by the rhythm and accuracy of the upswing. Golf is a recoil action, like chopping down a tree.

If a logger takes his 15-pound axe back all skew-whiff he cannot deliver the blade accurately to his target. Since a golf club is so much lighter, it is possible to make adjustments and corrections, as Nicklaus and Barnes have been demonstrating for years, but it is obviously preferable if you can play without having to add compensating movements to the swing.

End of lesson. The pupils are dismissed but I would like the staff to remain behind for a private word. At the Toski clinic I was reminded once more of how complicated you teachers are making the game. It is not that the things which you are teaching are wrong, far from it, but it seems to me that you are confusing the pupils by impressing on them things which are unnecessary for them to know.

Take the left heel. I have never been at a teaching session in which the professor did not lay great stress on the need to raise the left heel on the backswing. Instinctively, on hearing this advice, every person in the audience begins to fidget, raising his left heel and waggling his hips as if learning a new dance routine. Now there have been some fine flat-footed golfers – if I am not mistaken, Arnaud Massy and Ted Ray both played like this. However, I agree that most good golfers' heels do raise on the backswing but note my words. The heel raises; it is not raised.

In future, what I would like you to do is this. Once you have given the pupils an effective grip and a good set-up position, fill your lungs and shout at the top of your voice: 'FORGET ALL ABOUT YOUR BLOODY LEFT HEEL!' You might add, if you suspect that any of them have been guilty of reading instruction books: 'Forget about pointing your left knee at the ball at the backswing, forget about weight shift, forget about hip position.'

You all know, better than I do, that if the player makes a proper shoulder turn then all these lower body movements occur quite naturally in the classical style. They are not the cause of a good swing, they are the effect of a good turn.

By the same token, if you have a pupil whose left knee shoots straight forward when he makes his backswing, do not try to make him change his leg action. That is just treating the symptom, like dabbing iodine on measles spots. Look to his shoulder turn for that is the source of his faulty leg action. (In this case he is tilting.)

The game is difficult enough without making it more complicated than necessary.

The Observer, 1981

It's all in the mind

Once upon a time, when my daughters were young enough to be conned into pulling my trolley around a golf course for the promise of a chocolate bar and a fizzy drink, I took them both out one day for nine holes. In order to give them some small interest in proceedings, I played two balls on the basis that this one is yours and that one is hers. Ball A immediately went two up and, in the cause of equality, I sought to contrive that the two balls should finish all square. I tried very hard on every shot with Ball B and simply gave Ball A a carefree swat. At the end of nine holes Ball A was six up.

Everyone who plays golf has had such experiences, hitting superb shots while not trying. What happens next is that the astonished golfer seeks to repeat that wonder shot. He concentrates and the stroke is a disappointment. If at first you don't succeed . . . the harder he tries the worse the results.

Timothy Gallwey, the American tennis coach, observed similar oddities in his pupils and he thought deeply about the mental blockages which prevented people from performing simple actions of which they were perfectly capable.

The result of his researches was a book, *The Inner Game of Tennis*, which challenged traditional coaching methods and produced spectacular results. He has now transposed those techniques into the key of golf and I would like to think that *The Inner Game of Golf*

(Jonathan Cape, £5.95) will similarly stand golf instruction on its head.

During his rare excursions on to the golf course he did what we all do, telling himself to keep the left arm straight, to watch out for the trees down the left and to keep his eye on the ball. When he sliced he berated himself with the usual harangue: 'You lifted your head, you dummy.'

He asked himself who this arrogant, know-all voice belonged to and to whom it was speaking. The answer, obviously, was 'himself' in both cases and so if there was a dialogue he must have two selves. He called them Self One and Self Two and his whole inner game philosophy is based on his findings that Self Two is perfectly capable of performing the natural actions of hitting tennis or golf balls, provided that the expert, Smart Aleck Self One, can be prevented from fouling up the action by barking out his sergeant-major instructions.

Teaching golf by a sequence of imperatives – you must grip the club like this, stand like this, take the club back like this – is like teaching someone to say 'Severiano Ballesteros' by means of charts showing the tongue position for each syllable. It would take a lifetime and it would not work. It cannot be taught but it can be learnt from experience, the way a child learns to walk.

What saves Gallwey's book from being just another dose of shrinkery is that he is a pragmatist. Every step of the way he provides practical exercises so the reader can put his ideas to the test.

The first exercise is an adaptation of his basic tennis teaching. Go to the practice ground and do not worry about results. As your club reaches the top of the backswing you say out loud 'back'. Then, as the club-head contacts the ball you say 'hit'. The actual words do not matter. The purpose is to eliminate the interference from Self One and since Self Two is the one who does the talking, Self One is submerged.

An extension of this exercise is to focus your attention on the position of the club-head through the swing. You do not concern yourself with where it ought to be, just with where it is. Similarly, you do not try to correct errors in your shots. You observe that the ball slices, for instance, but you make no conscious effort to apply a technical adjustment. That is Self One's department and the whole point is to keep him out of the action. Self Two will receive feedback from the sight of the slice and he will learn from the experience without any conscious effort on your part. Thus the stumbling baby learns to walk.

Tension is the enemy of the golfer. There are two ways you can learn to relax on your shots. At the address you tighten every muscle as hard as you can, gripping the club with all your might. Then you relax everything and start your swing.

You can also hum as you swing. I suggest waltz time to induce a languid tempo. Now, if you tense up as the club approaches impact that tension will result in a change of pitch in your humming. Self Two will get the message and you will soon be humming and swinging harmoniously.

There is perhaps just room for a word or two about Gallwey's solution to self-doubt. You have a tricky putt or a tight drive and doubt your ability to make the shot. So you become tense and impair your ability to make the shot.

The answer is to associate the difficult shot with a mental image of something easy. On the putt you think about picking the ball out of the hole, which is easy enough. For the tight drive you might think of throwing a cricket ball through that 30-yard gap, which is an action you would perform confidently. By associating the difficult problem with a simple solution you reduce the difficulty.

There is much, much more and if I cannot go along all the way with Gallwey's thesis that learning should completely displace teaching (I believe that a modicum of expert advice can greatly speed the learning process) I heartily commend this book to golfers of every level, not excluding experienced tournament professionals. For absolute beginners it offers an exciting alternative to the traditional grind of lessons from the pro because it is a method of learning golf without trying. That is the essential message: trying fails.

The Observer, 1981

Of yippers, twitchers and jitterers

Apart from being beaned by errant golf balls, assaulted by peevish golfers who resent being described in print as choppers, incurring curvature of the spine through being cramped up in cheap charter flights and suffering lurid stomach disorders from foreign cuisine, the main occupational hazards of the golf correspondent are scrivener's palsy and writer's block.

You don't want to hear about my problems. You have troubles of your own. But wait. Scrivener's palsy is out to get all of us who play golf. Otherwise known as writer's cramp, it afflicts the pen-holding hand with a rigour which precludes any function more legible than the trail of a drunken spider which has fallen into the ink pot. The palsy in turn induces writer's block, a condition which turns the patient into a dull-eyed zombie who sits staring for hours at a blank sheet of paper and cursing the biological bulldozer which has severed all lines of communication to the brain.

The same fate awaits golfers, which is why I am glad to see that medical science is at last taking this form of hysteria with due seriousness in the person of Dr Wolfgang Schady, consultant lecturer in neurology at Manchester University. He has just addressed the British Association on the subject known variously as the Yips, the Twitch, the Staggers, the Waggles, the Jitters, or just Them.

The Twitch apparently is one of a group of disorders known as occupational cramps and victims include violinists, telegraphists and, frightful thought, milkers. 'Hold on, Daisy. I'll just do some finger-flexing exercises and we'll try again.'

The late Henry Longhurst was a sufferer from the Twitch and the experience of taking three putts from a yard on the 18th green at St Andrews was the final indignity which caused him to give up the game which he had graced and loved all his life.

He wrote what I have always considered to be the definitive description of the Yip Syndrome, with a grim catalogue of case histories. Thus Tommy Armour: 'That ghastly time when, with the first movement of the putter, the golfer blacks out, loses sight of the ball and hasn't the remotest idea of what to do with the putter or, occasionally, that he is holding a putter at all.'

Or Harry Vardon, who once lost the US Open by missing a one-inch putt: 'As I stood addressing the ball I would watch for my right hand to jump. At the end of two seconds I would not be looking at the ball at all. My gaze would have become riveted on my right hand. I simply could not resist the desire to see what it was going to do. Directly, as I felt that it was about to jump, I would snatch at the ball in a desperate effort to play the shot before the involuntary movement could take effect. Up would go my head and body with a start and off would go the ball, anywhere but on the proper line.'

The Twitch has ended the career of many a good man. Wild Bill Mehlhorn was finished after he jerked a three-footer clear across the green into a bunker. Craig Wood finally had to accept that perseverance was useless against this destructive malady. Peter Alliss was

77

one of the most gifted players I have ever seen, up to about 5 feet from the hole. Those last few excruciating inches did for him when he was in his prime, prematurely ending his distinguished career. The same goes double for Ben Hogan.

Many remedies have been tried but mostly they proved to be no more than palliatives. Leo Diegel's spread-elbow style merely postponed the inevitable. Cross-handed grips, spread-handed styles, often with the right hand down on the hosel, one-handed with 12-inch putters, index finger down the shaft (currently favoured by Mark James) and putting with the eyes closed have all been advocated from time to time.

Sam Snead, among others, found a new lease of golfing life with the croquet method until the United States Golf Association banned standing astride the line of the putt. Snead adapted the croquet method with his sidewinder style, not with outstanding success but at least it enabled him to make a controlled stroke.

Armour theorised that the Yips were a tournament disease, the result of years of competitive strain which produced a sort of punch-nuttiness with the putter. Longhurst challenged that conclusion, rightly pointing out that the disorder was common among ordinary club golfers who never played serious competitive golf.

Where I take issue with Longhurst is in his bleak conclusion that 'Once you've had 'em, you've got 'em' and I am encouraged in this opinion by Dr Schady, despite the fact that a member of his department at Manchester has developed a pen which delivers an electric shock whenever scrivener's palsy sets in.

'Such Pavlovian methods have not been used on golfers afflicted with the Yips, perhaps because an electrified golf club sounds vaguely threatening [I love that "vaguely"] and would probably be illegal.'

Nevertheless there is hope, as the example of Bernhard Langer shows. As a teenager he had the worst case of Yips I have ever seen and yet today he is at the top of the European Tour's putting statistics with an average below 30. This is the man who used to rejoice on the rare occasions when he did not have a four-putt green in his round.

One cause of the Yips, I am convinced, is that some golfers' vision of the hole does not coincide with its actual position. They are always aiming at a target which isn't there. Langer, for instance, has severe astigmatism in one eye and he has at last learned to lay off his aim to accommodate the disorder, directing his putts at a phantom hole, in truth the real hole, wide of the one he sees.

If an eye test fails to cure the Yips, then Dr Schady's advice to use a different technique is sound, so far as it goes. My conclusion is that the Twitch afflicts the small muscles of the fingers and hands and that salvation lies in taking them out of the action. Clamp the arms to the side and immobilise the hands and wrists on the grip. Now move the club-head with a lateral shimmy of the hips. It looks odd, as if Twitchers care about that, but it does work. And once the short putts start to drop regularly normal service is gradually restored to the hands and the patient can return to his normal method. Try it; you have nothing to lose but the match.

The Observer, 1984

Terrors of the pro-am

Everybody knows that the greatest glory of the game of golf is a handicapping system that enables the veriest rabbit to play on level terms with Jack Nicklaus. Everybody who has actually put this glory to the test knows it to be a load of cobblers.

However, since there is only one Jack Nicklaus and at a rough count there are some 30–40 million rabbits, the myth survives and there is never any shortage of romantic fools who believe that their handicap strokes make them the equal of the star tournament players.

Hence the pro-am, a highly refined form of golf torture whose only merit is that it raises millions and millions of pounds for charity every year.

A non-golfer with a keen grasp of higher mathematics will tell you that the handicap system is foolproof. A 16-handicapper will, by definition, play 16 strokes more than par and if he gets his full stroke allowance, as mostly happens in pro-ams, he will have a 72, which is likely to be the score of his pro.

In practice it does not work like that. What happens is that as soon as the 16-handicapper learns that he has been drawn to play with Sandy Lyle he breaks into a cold sweat. Strictly speaking he is clinically mad from now on with a mental derangement known to psychiatrists as Toad of Toad Hall syndrome. The syndrome includes severe dislocation from reality, fantasies about playing a career best round of 73, less 16, giving a net 57, probably followed by a request from the admiring Lyle to come to the practice ground and pass on a few tips.

The disease now follows a predictable pattern. The victim goes to the pro's shop and splurges on a new colour co-ordinated outfit of shirt, sweater, slacks, glove, cap, pro bag and, the first fatal error, new shoes. The second really disastrous mistake is that he also books up for a lesson. Having guaranteed that he will suffer from blistered heels and that his limited ability will have deteriorated by a minimum of 10 strokes a round, he is now ready for the big day.

When they meet on the first tee Lyle could not be more comforting. 'Just play your normal game and don't worry about anything. We'll have a nice, friendly round.' Our poor booby tries to reply but owing to the dryness of his throat his merry quip comes out as a Donald Duck croak. There are, he estimates, some 10,000 spectators gathered around the first tee, all of them wearing expressions of mocking amusement.

Something very peculiar is happening to his knees. His name is called and he tees his ball. A sudden spasm afflicts his hands and the ball falls off the tee. Someone in the gallery titters. By the time he straightens up his hands are trembling uncontrollably, a problem for which there is only one solution. He grasps the driver in a grip so tight that all circulation of blood below the wrist is thwarted. It has to go somewhere and, as he addresses the ball, a red glaze covers his eyes, effectively blinding him. His rising panic is compounded by the sudden realisation that he has forgotten what he is supposed to do with the golf club. Some vestigial instinct prompts him to raise the driver in the manner of a drunken executioner lifting his sword; in a convulsive spasm he brings it down again. The toe of the driver catches the ball a glancing blow, causing it to shoot off at a right angle and inflict painful shin wounds among the sneering populace.

That tangential cover drive from the first tee is a common opening gambit in pro-ams but there are several interesting variations: the air shot, the scuttling squirt into the left rough, the swing which passes clean underneath the ball in a flurry of flying turf and tee peg, leaving the ball to drop vertically into the crater. My own speciality used to be the premature evacuation, with the club-head entering the turf 11 inches (my personal best) behind the ball and ploughing onwards with a growing accumulation of grass and dirt pushed by my impromptu bulldozer blade just far enough to topple the ball from its peg.

Renton Laidlaw of the *London Standard* pioneered an elegant variation on this gambit, his club-head stopping two inches short of its target, having neatly curled a divot right over the ball which sat

there undisturbed beneath its leafy canopy. (He then uncurled the divot, stamped it flat and hit a whizzer down the fairway, although I have always maintained that he should have penalised himself for improving his lie.)

Anyway, once the pantomime of the opening tee shot is over things tend to improve and, speaking of penalties, the pro-am amateur should lose no opportunity to pull the integrity ploy. Once you are sure your score cannot contribute to the team's fortunes, call a penalty on yourself, whether or not it is justified, ostentatiously put your ball away and announce: 'I'm afraid you chaps will have to do the business on this hole. Damn ball moved at the address.' You thus create the impression of honest endeavour thwarted by bad luck and, incidentally, contribute to the speed of play.

Salvage your esteem

If you are of a certain age you can further salvage your esteem within the group by steering the conversation around to the war. Inevitably, someone will mention an item of military hardware, such as the Scharnhorst or the Tiger or the Junkers 87. That's your opening. You snort: 'Don't talk to me about Stukas; I've spent the last 40 years trying to forget the damn things.' Then you walk quickly away, trying hard not to limp.

By such conversational strategies the experienced pro-am hand can contribute not a single point to the team's welfare but win the reputation as a frightfully decent chap, brave, modest and cheerful even though he was dreadfully unlucky with the golf. Obviously a pretty useful player but it was just not his day.

The identity of the professional introduces an element of lottery into pro-ams. If you can afford it, the best plan is to bribe the officials to team you with the pro of your choice. Otherwise, the day can be a disaster. I once had to play with an Italian assistant and three amateurs of the same nationality, not one of whom spoke a word of English nor, as far as I could judge, had a passing acquaintance with the laws of the game. At the other end of the scale the best pro by far was Max Faulkner who kept us in enthralled hysterics with ribald anecdotes about famous players. He also gave the impression that the sole purpose of the day was to cure our faults and he gave us each a lesson before every shot. His own golf was purely incidental. 'I'll just give this a swish.' By the end we were all hitting the ball quite respectably. I think he scored a 67.

Tommy Horton and Brian Barnes are inheritors of this tradition but not every pro is quite so amenable. That is understandable. Just imagine that you have missed four cuts in a row, the bank manager is making hostile noises and, owing to a mechanical failure of your car, it's your only chance to study and pace the course before the tournament. You explain all this before the round and crave the indulgence of your amateurs, promising to chat as much as they like between holes. Off you go, measuring the distance to the front of the green: 176, 177, 178, 179 – 'I say, pro, what's Arnold Palmer really like?' 'Eh?' 'I mean, he comes across as a nice guy on TV but I wondered if that was all a front.' 'No, he is a nice guy. Excuse me a minute, I'm counting out my yardage. Now where the hell was I? 205, 206, 207. . . .'

Most pros have a litany of automatic responses which they can utter without breaking their train of thought. The sound of club-head making solid contact with a ball prompts the reflex 'Hey! Who's the pro in this group?' as automatically as a 'pardon' after a belch. Bernard Gallacher, bless him, has developed a brilliant strategy. Every time an amateur asks 'What club should I take?' Gallacher answers 'three-wood', even if the ball is on the fringe of the green. The beauty of that system is that it absolves him of all necessity for thought and his advice always results in a satisfactory shot.

The real pleasure of pro-ams is not to be found in showing off your golfing talent but in being able to observe at close quarters the extraordinary skills of the pro. And if you can persuade him to show off, especially if he is a magician like Severiano Ballesteros, the participation in a pro-am becomes the golfing experience of the amateur's life.

The other lasting satisfaction of participating in pro-ams comes later, when you are back at the club with a lifetime's ammunition for boring the pants off your friends. 'I shall never forget when I was playing with Queenie, that's what all his friends call Michael King, and he said that with my swing if I could devote an hour a day to my golf I could get down to scratch in six months. . . .'

Golf World, 1983

Going with the grain

When is it correct to have a square peg in a round hole? That was the question put to me by Bert Williamson, who is now the pro at the Is Molas club in Sardinia. Having known Bert as a fine player and teacher and club-maker I should have been able to make a stab at the answer but I must confess that I was nonplussed, as I expect most of you must be.

The answer is in making wooden-headed golf clubs in the traditional manner, a craft which has almost vanished although Laurie Auchterlonie in St Andrews still fashions superb wooden-headed putters using the methods and materials which originated in the days of the Stuart kings.

In shaping the head from persimmon a groove is cut from the front edge of the sole to take an insert of ram's horn. This protects the club from scuffs as it contacts the ground. Having cut the insert of horn and shaped it by immersion in boiling water, so that it fits snugly into its groove, holes (usually three) are bored in a cunning manner. Once the drill bit has penetrated through the horn into the wood, the drill is canted, so that the hole is slightly angled. Now the groove is glued, the horn insert replaced, and square pegs are dipped into the glue-pot and hammered home.

Metal sole plates superseded the ram's horn inserts and the heads themselves evolved from the long-nosed shape to squatter, rounder forms at about the same time that club-makers began drilling holes in the neck to fit the shafts instead of glueing them with a scare.

These are minor innovations for four centuries of progress and even though machines have largely replaced the craftsmen, and steel has taken over from hickory for the shafts, the wooden clubs we use today are in the tradition of the implements used by the pioneers of the game.

Wood is surely the noblest natural material used by man. Wood elevated man above the apes in the form of a club and the affinity has grown stronger down the centuries as man adapted wood for his home, his transport, his defence, his livelihood, his furniture and his decoration, not to mention his fuel.

No wonder we all respond to wood. With our heritage we could not help ourselves and I dare say that this feeling for wood accounts for the fact that we go on using it (gun stocks, Morris Minor estates), where other materials would be more appropriate. We even touch wood for luck and you cannot get much more atavistic than that.

Golfers like wood. There is nothing in golf quite to compare with the feeling of cracking a ball dead off the meat of a wooden club. We become irrationally attached to wooden clubs. My own driver has a head older than I am. It is a nice piece of persimmon and don't ask me why I describe it as 'nice'; the description just seems incomplete without the adjective.

I have long since lost track of the number of times it has been into the shop for repairs and refurbishing and re-shafting. The development of epoxy glues and fillers came along just in time to give that head a new lease of life and it must be a matter for conjecture which of us falls to pieces first.

Pros fall in love (the only appropriate expression) with wooden clubs. I remember the tenderness in Graham Marsh's voice and the light in his eyes when he told me that he had found a driver. He had been rummaging among some old clubs in the back of a pro's shop when their eyes met across the dusty room and the massed strings of Mantovani's orchestra began to play. Personally I thought the club to be a raddled old hag, bulging in all the wrong places and retaining hardly a speck of varnish on her battered person.

'Just wait,' said Graham like a golfing Professor Higgins, 'and see what I can make of her.' That nice piece of persimmon was given the works and I did not recognise her when he drew off the head cover and unveiled a stunning beauty. To the best of my knowledge he has not given a glance to another driver since then and their union has been blessed by many first prizes.

Marsh is not an exception. Many tournament players would sell their grandmothers rather than part with their favourite woods. Many, but not all. A quiet revolution has begun in the golf club business, as you may have noticed in the telecast of the US Open championship from Pebble Beach. On the last day a close-up of Bruce Devlin's driver on the 18th tee revealed that it was not made of wood at all. The head was a shell of stainless steel.

In the Coral Classic at Royal Porthcawl Carl Mason gave credit for his fine scoring to a metal four-wood. The American Tom Sieckman started the fashion in Europe, driving prodigious distances with his 'Pittsburgh Persimmon' metal-wood driver.

Today I suppose one pro in 20 carries at least one metal-wood club and the proportion is rising. What the professional does today the club golfer is sure to do tomorrow, especially as the magic property ascribed to metal-woods is that they hit the ball farther.

They are extremely practical, since they do not swell in the wet, or lose their screws, or chip, or need varnishing, or scratch, or lose their whipping. They are here to stay, for they represent genuine progress, and I have to admit that I have one. So far I have not used it. As I write it is standing against the wall, seemingly mocking me with its flash, shiny face and challenging my loyalty. No doubt I shall fall to temptation and give it a try but it will go against the grain.

The Observer, 1982

Cut down on the hardware

In an extensive stable of golfing hobby-horses my favourite is Short Set. I am fond of all of them, of course, and enjoy an exhilarating canter on Brisk Play, Five-inch Hole, Banish Carts, Simplify Rules, Organic Turf Culture, Nicklaus the Greatest and Miss 'em Quick, and there are a number of other promising colts and fillies in the yard, but Short Set, by *Idée Fixe* out of Obsession, is a hobby-horse in a million.

She is a real thoroughbred with an impeccable pedigree. Remember how Harry Vardon won six Open championships with Short Set? And never forget that Bobby Jones romped home in the only Grand Slam in the history of golf with Short Set. Those were yesterday's glories, it is true, and since the introduction of the 14-club rule Short Set has rather fallen from public favour.

The notion has grown up that because 14 clubs are permissible so 14 clubs are necessary. That is a ridiculous idea and a slur on the unrivalled achievements of Short Set. My mission in life is to restore Short Set's noble reputation so I was delighted to find support for her from an unexpected quarter, a golf club manufacturer. Generally speaking the trade has engaged in a campaign of vilification against Short Set. For venal commercial reasons the club makers have promoted the virtues of Full Set. In fact Full Set is a grotesque caricature with more than a hint of camel in the breeding. Full Set purports to be four woods, irons numbered from one to nine, pitching wedge, sand wedge and putter. Just look at that conformation; it adds up to 16 clubs. Dammit, Full Set is illegitimate. You have to amputate bits of Full Set before you can take the nag onto the course. You need a portmanteau of a bag to accommodate Full Set, then a caddie or a trolley to transport the elephantine brute.

The worst vice of Full Set, however, is that it reduces golf to a mere repetition of a standard stroke and thereby eliminates half the challenge and appeal of the game. The trade support for Short Set, mentioned earlier, is from the Demiset company which has brought out a set consisting of nine clubs. Most adherents of Short Set golf normally use only the odd numbered clubs from Full Set or, as in my own case, pick up a mongrel collection of strays and hammer the lofts and lies into a theoretically effective progression. The problem was that I hit the six-iron further than the 4½-iron because it was a much better club and compatible with what I rather pretentiously call my swing.

With this properly designed Short Set there are no such idiosyncrasies. It consists of two woods, 1½-wood and 3½-wood although I must admit that I would prefer them to be given names rather than numbers. Let us call them driver and spoon. There are five irons, ranging from 2½ to 8½ under the numerical system. What this means is that the player can span the range normally covered by seven or eight clubs. Surely, you may object, this leaves awkward gaps when you feel yourself to be between clubs, too near for the four-iron and too far for the 5½. Not at all. You might feel like that, provided you are a player of such consistency that you can group your shots within a 3-yard circle. With Full Set golf the spread between clubs is 12 yards; with Short Set it is 15 yards. So what? The only difference is that with Short Set you have more and better opportunities to grip the club half an inch shorter, and to play three-quarter shots, and to exercise your full repertory of cut-up strokes, punch shots, low fades and high hooks. A double duty wedge and a putter complete the armoury and I insist that this is all a golfer could or should ever need.

Not least of the joys of Short Set golf is that, with a lightweight bag, I can grasp the clubs at the point of balance in one hand and hold them with outstretched arm without a tremor of exertion. Offer me an attractive bet and I will hold them like this for a full minute. For double or quits I will undertake to throw them over the trolley shed roof like a spear. If the money is right I will lie down and you can drop this bag of clubs on my belly from a height of 6 feet.

The benefits which flow from this lightness are reflected in my scores. With a conventional cabin trunk full of ironmongery, plus a wardrobe of spare clothing in the pockets, I am a prime victim of the Elderly Golfer Syndrome. The pattern of this dire malady will be familiar with most golfers of my generation: it takes nine holes to work the kinks out of your spine and to free the ball and socket joints in the shoulder. Then, nicely loosened, you hit one good shot, usually the approach to the ninth green. By the time you climb on to the 10th tee the strain of lugging all that equipment about begins to tell and the quality of your play deteriorates. You are knackered and by the end of the round you are absolutely knackered. Results: you score 108 and explain to your mates that your putting was off.

Short Set fortifies the over forties. Carrying nine clubs in a light bag is no burden. You can walk along tossing the bag from hand to hand if you like and after 18 holes you still feel so fresh that you can scamper up the clubhouse steps and indulge your natural generosity by getting in the first round.

Golf World, 1982

Love thy putter

Although golf was played in the Middle Ages, the game at that time was not complicated by billiard-table greens. You had to putt into a hole, or so we assume, but since you scooped a pinch of sand out of the hole to make a tee for your next drive, and you had to play from within a club's length of the hole, we may conjecture that the putting was mostly a case of chipping over some pretty rough territory and then tapping the ball in when you got it close.

That was just as well, for if putters of the calibre of Bobby Locke, Bob Charles, Jack Nicklaus and Ben Crenshaw had been around in those days, coolly knocking them in from all over the place, the superstitious citizenry would have dragged them off and burned them at the stake as wizards.

Putting is still a black art. There is no right way to putt. Good putters have feel or touch, and do not ask me what that means, or why it happens, because nobody knows. We have all enjoyed that mystical experience of walking up to a long putt and knowing that it is going to dart straight into the hole. That is a case of pure feel triumphing over method but feel is ephemeral. One day you've got it and the next time out the putter hefts like a sledgehammer in your hands and you can't even threaten the hole.

The conventional reaction on such occasions is to switch putters, trying a lighter or heavier model but persisting with your normal style. The remedy I would like to suggest is to adopt a drastically different method of putting, and it works just as well for sufferers from the yips as it does for those demented golfers who have temporarily lost all their feel on the greens.

Here is what you do. At every golf club on an average of about once a week a member comes into the pro's shop clutching the separate components of a club that has broken, the shaft having snapped at the junction with the hosel. The pro fits a new shaft but, and here is your opportunity, he has a collection of shafts complete with grip lying about in his workshop. Beg one from him. If necessary offer him 25 cents and pick a good long one, preferably from a one-iron or a wood.

Now allow your imagination full rein. What can you use for a head? The opportunities are boundless, anything from a piece of polished driftwood to a glass paperweight. Fashion this head with care and love until you are suffused with pride at your handiwork. Have a hole drilled to take the shaft so that the finished club has a very upright lie, not more than 10 degrees out of vertical. You will need another hole opposite your intended sweet spot to add weight. Unless you are experienced with using molten metals do not mess with amateur foundry work. Use lead shot and secure it in place with epoxy glue, adding the pellets bit by bit until the club feels exactly right for you.

Do not rush the job. The more painstaking work you put into making your putter, the more magic you will impart into it.

Your beautiful creation should be long enough so that you can address the ball comfortably while standing perfectly upright. Many sufferers treat their putting problems by bending lower and lower over the ball, sometimes going to the extremes of using ludicrously short putters. That is exactly the opposite of my suggested treatment, for the closer you get to the ball, the more you have to employ the small muscles of hand and wrist, which are the ones most susceptible to nervous tremor. My idea is to eliminate these treacherous small muscles altogether, because they are the destructive influences that give the golfer the frightening notion that he is putting with a live snake.

So, stand up tall and proud, with arms absolutely straight and with a firm (but not tense and rigid) grip with the left hand. Your left arm and club now form what is in effect a pendulum, free to swing from the shoulder, in one straight line. The only function of the left hand in this method is to hold the club, with never a hint of hingeing of the wrist. The thought to bear in mind is that the right hand will draw back this elongated club/arm and then push it back through the ball, with the directional control guided by the palm of the right hand. You should feel that you are slapping the ball towards the hole with the palm of the right hand.

You can use this long putter with a rocking movement of the shoulders although I favour emphasizing the feeling that the left arm/club is a solid entity swinging freely from a stationary left shoulder.

In really virulent cases of the yips, in which the patient cannot keep control of the club-head with a right-handed push, an effective stroke can be made with the long putter by keeping the arms entirely rigid and moving the club-head with a sliding motion of the hips. It is not a good putting method but it does at least allow the yipper to make a stroke of some sort. Once he has regained a semblance of confidence, he should be able to progress to more effective styles. In putting, confidence is everything. If the long-putter method gives you confidence, then you can revert any time you want to the wonderful range of putters available in your pro's shop.

Golf World, 1975

Chapter 4

On a point of law,
your honour

Caught by conscience

It is astonishing how often, when playing against an opponent who has never before observed me in action, he will make some remark such as: 'Funny, I thought you would be at least a scratch player.' If the stranger happens to be my partner, the same observation is usually made in rather more caustic terms. 'Jeeeez! And to think you have devoted your entire adult life to this game. Tom Fazio must have had you in mind when he built a bunker behind the first tee at Lake Nona.'

A dignified silence is the only proper response to such ill-mannered remarks. I am, as it happens, potentially a superb striker of the golf ball and a brilliant tactician and since you, dear reader, have not insulted me I shall explain why that latent talent is never revealed on the golf course.

This game, as everyone knows, is based on concentration. Without giving your full attention to the job in hand, golf is unplayable. My problem is that I am constantly distracted by nagging doubts over the legality of my equipment. How I envy you fortunate golfers who are content to scan the notice board to confirm that the ball you are about to use is on the Approved List. That is not good enough for conscientious chaps like me. We take our responsibilities seriously. We want to cross-check every detail personally so that we can play with an easy mind.

There is only one way to do that: go to Golf House in Far Hills, New Jersey, and say: 'Would you be so kind as to confirm that the velocity of this Pinnacle X-out does not exceed 76.2 metres per second within a tolerance of 2 per cent when measured on your apparatus at a temperature within the range of 22 and 24 degrees Centigrade? I would hate to obtain an undue advantage over my opponent by using a rogue ball.' They would throw a net over you and send for the men in the white coats.

So we sticklers for fair play are at a terrible disadvantage. You tee up a ball and try to hit it while worrying yourself sick because you do not understand what is meant by 'Maximum Absolute Difference of the Means'. Whatever it is, you do not have the slightest idea whether the ball will conform to the necessary 0.9 grid units, whatever they might be.

Your cocoon of concentration is penetrated by an impatient cough from your opponent. Must press on. You start your takeaway. As you reach the top, another terrifying thought transfixes your pulsating brain: 'If in two successive tests differences in the same two or more measurements are statistically significant at the 5 per cent level of significance and exceed the limits set forth below, the ball type will not conform to the symmetry specification.' What on earth can it mean? What they seem to be saying is that if my Pinnacle X-out measures 1.68 inches and then I measure it again and it comes out at 1.59 inches, then I am cheating.

But such a phenomenon could only occur if my ball were physically changing shape before my very eyes, like a throbbing heart. The only pragmatic test I can apply in the circumstances is to sneak a quick peek at the ball – not a bad thing to do, at the top of the backswing, according to the experts.

Extraordinary! Incredible! The ball really is changing shape. It is also going in and out of focus, one minute appearing to be a shiny white pea and then ballooning up to the size and texture of a furry tennis ball. The image of a new-born chick covered in pristine, white down and doing deep breathing exercises comes irresistibly to mind.

Call me a sentimental old fool if you like, but humane instincts take over. Not only am I cheating by using an illegal ball but I am about to snuff out the miracle of life. The accelerating club-head is arrested by plunging into the turf a foot behind the ball. Impact is cushioned by a huge divot and the baby chick takes its first, halting flight before alighting just short of the ladies' tee. It makes no sound so I emit a squeak of anguish on its behalf.

On behalf of all decent, honest and like-minded golfers who want to play golf strictly by the book, I appeal to the authorities to revise the book and give us back the true game of golf. Out of consideration for the manufacturers and their stock holders, announce now the following revisions – or restorations – for the 1992 rules:-

1)   Minimum size of the ball to be increased to 2 inches in diameter. Within that constraint the ball-makers can do what they like. The effect of this reform would be to restore all those wonderful Ross, Tillinghast and Mackenzie courses to their former glory.

2)   Club-makers to submit designs for approval under the traditional form-and-make rule, the ruling bodies to be the sole arbiters. On receiving approval the club-maker shall be licensed to stamp every club with a distinguishing mark of approval.

3)   All woods shall have heads made of wood.

4)   Give notice that as from the beginning of the 21st century, face markings on irons shall be limited to decorative sand blasting.

That little lot would eliminate some of the gibberish from the rule book and do for starters. Then they could start trimming the superfluous complexities from the rules of play.

Golf World, 1990

Golf a la cart

The barbarians are within the gate. Civilization is teetering on the brink of the abyss.

It may be presumptuous for a foreigner, albeit a one-time resident and still a frequent visitor, to criticize American institutions, but regular readers would be shocked if this column suddenly started to display good manners.

What American institution, you ask, is the churlish old curmudgeon fulminating against this time? Well, it is not my present purpose to deplore the demise of the corner drugstore, that temple of American life where all right-thinking citizens used to make their morning devotions, to exchange gossip and compose their minds against the rigours of the day. Is it a coincidence that when the drugstores were torn down they were replaced by psychoanalysis surgeries?

Nor is this going to be a nostalgic requiem for the local bar, now surviving only as a terminally boring TV soap opera.

Mention of terminal boredom may prompt the suspicion that this is going to be the usual limey moan about America taking perfectly good English games and ruining them. Not at all. Football is clearly designed by and for television to numb the minds of viewers so that they will be receptive to the contrasting excitement of the advertisements. And just in case someone might begin to get an inkling about what is happening in the play, TV has devised those explanatory diagrams to restore total confusion. Besides, football contributes a useful social service by providing gainful employment for a vast number of psychopaths who would otherwise be causing untold mayhem in the streets.

Furthermore, this is not going to be a howl of protest at the profanity of Italian–American restaurants banishing spaghetti from their menus. Apparently the glory of Italian cuisine has become déclassé because of its truck-stop associations with spaghetti and meatballs.

We are at last closing in on the subject of this column's disapproval, however, because it also involves a down-market, municipal golf course class of object: the pullcart.

Since caddies are a vanishing breed, and golf's governing bodies stubbornly shirk their clear duty to limit the permitted number of clubs to 10, thereby making the shouldering of your clubs a physical impossibility for all but the youngest and fittest, a pullcart is the obvious answer.

This is where the barbarians came in. They either forbade the use of pullcarts outright, or propounded the snobbish doctrine that they were vulgar and not suitable at a 'good' golf club. The result is that golf courses have become disfigured by the varicose veins of blacktop cartpaths and golfers are obliged to pay heavily for motorized carts.

The time has come to reassert some basic principles. Golf is a pedestrian game. No golf course that is scarred by cartpaths can lay claim to greatness. When the temperature is below 90 degrees nobody, except the infirm, who trundle around in carts, can call himself a golfer.

When Sandy Tatum was president of the US Golf Association he spelled all this out most eloquently and proposed that those who insisted on riding carts should find a new name for their activity. His suggestion was 'cart ball'.

The case for pedestrian golf owes nothing to stuffy tradition and the good old days. Its validity lies in the nature of the game itself. Golf is designed to provide healthy exercise. It offers the opportunity to refresh the spirit through the tranquil enjoyment of the natural beauty of the countryside. Walking pace provides the proper tempo to absorb and analyse the strategic qualities of the course. These are all essential elements of the game, perhaps the greater parts of it.

The cart destroys them; the pullcart, or trolley, retains them. If the physical labour of pulling a trolley is beneath the dignity of the country club set, there is an aristocrat breed among trolleys, the electric version, that rolls along at the touch of a button, making you feel as though you are accompanied by a well-trained pedigree Irish wolfhound.

This is not so much a call to arms as a call to legs. Arise, golfers of America, and insist on your rights. Rediscover the satisfactions of real golf. After all, you have nothing to lose but your excess poundage, your incipient heart attacks and your extortionate cart fees.

Golf Digest, 1991

Bigger is beautiful

Some months ago I timorously advanced the suggestion that golf might be a better game if the hole were slightly larger. It was by no means an original idea, for I am quite sure that ever since the day when two anonymous Dutchmen devised the game of golf there have been arguments about the size of the hole.

It was only by sheer accident that golf came to be played with a hole at all. Club and ball games had been played ever since the days of the Roman Empire. In Europe during the Middle Ages these games had taken different forms but were mostly played to marks such as barn doors and haystacks. The Dutch formalized these targets into ornately carved and painted posts and, since these posts were precious objects, it was the custom to remove them after play for safekeeping, leaving a hole in the ground. We can conjecture that a twig or stick might have been left to mark the position of the hole to simplify the process of setting the post in place again.

Anyone who sneaked out in the evening to try his hand at this curious pastime would have had to play to the holes in the ground.

JAN (who had just lipped out a four-footer): I wish those kolfers would use bigger posts.

PIET (having chipped in from 5 yards): No, the posts are a perfect size. If they were any bigger they would be too heavy to carry.

So we inherited the most exquisite game ever devised by man, an exercise that combines the limits of physical exertion with the extremes of delicacy. Power and precision. Abandon and control. Muscle and mind. The ultimate confrontation between the will of man and his own infirmities of character. In no sport is the player brought face to face with his own inner weaknesses as in golf, especially when handling the putter.

Over the years I have come to believe that the arbitrary 4¼-inch hole is not quite big enough to serve the true purpose and enjoyment of golf. The letters I received suggest that there is a massive body of support for this view.

Broken hulks of men took pen in their palsied fingers and wrote: 'God bless you, squire. I was once a strapping athletic figure and fearless with it. During my vacations from my job as test pilot for atomic-powered backpacks I used to wrestle Bengal tigers, juggle live hand grenades while riding a unicycle on a tightrope stretched across Niagara Falls and take close-up photographs of Frank Sinatra for the gutter press. Then a friend introduced me to golf.

'I quickly got down to a plus-four handicap. In my club championship, on a really tough course during the height of Hurricane Hannah, I hit every fairway and every green in regulation and lagged every approach putt up to 3 feet. Each time I took extreme care and struck perfect second putts, dead on line and beautifully judged for pace. Would you believe that on 18 consecutive greens a spike mark deflected my putt wide of the hole for a 90?

'They are very kind to me here at the nursing home and the chief warden, who plays at the local public course on his day off, is understanding about what I did to the superintendent on that awful day. I enclose a piece of cloth that I made on the loom in the occupational therapy unit for you to use as a golf towel. Keep up your campaign and save others from the fate that befell me. Yours sincerely, Yippy the Mashie Murderer.'

My thesis is that if the hole were 5 inches in diameter it would be possible to strike putts at a pace that would ride over the blemishes that inevitably occur on even the best of greens and the putts would drop instead of catching on the back lip and jumping out. Good putters would still have the advantage over indifferent putters; superior strikers would be duly rewarded because hitting an approach shot to the green would give the player a positive edge over the player who missed the green (and who now gets down in a chip and putt).

Now a formidable champion in the cause of a larger hole has reappeared on the scene in the person of born-again golf nut Roy Canedy. He used to build and operate golf courses back in the 1950s and he devised a 4¾-inch liner. He ran successful and popular pro tournaments using the larger hole, and not least among the benefits was that play was speeded up by 30 minutes a round. Quite a few executive courses still use his liners to this day.

Canedy reminds me that when the United States Golf Association increased the size of the ball to 1.68 inches it did not enlarge the size of the hole in proportion, an omission that so enraged Gene Sarazen that he organized a tournament with 8-inch cups, popularly called Sarazen's Washtubs. Even so, Wild Bill Mehlhorn contrived to three-putt five times.

Implacable opposition from the USGA discouraged Canedy and he defected to ocean yachting. Now, however, his evangelical fervour for golf has returned and, with time and financial resources at his disposal, he is resuming the battle for acceptance of his 4¾-inch liners. He is setting up a corporation to manufacture and sell both the concept and the hardware of his larger hole. He believes that a groundswell of public opinion could force the ruling bodies into acceptance of that precious extra half-inch and cites the precedent of the Western Golf Association's defiance of authority in abolishing the stymie.

The idea of a larger hole is worthy and, in my view, a necessary reform in order to restore the proper balance of golf and to make tournament golf slightly less of a putting contest and more of a golf competition. However, I would much prefer the USGA to take the initiative. The determination of an ideal size hole would make a fascinating research subject, which the USGA is well equipped to handle, possibly in conjunction with experiments to increase the ball size slightly and thus maintain the playing character of the classic golf courses.

Unless my calculations are seriously astray, a 1.7-inch ball and a 5-inch hole would make for a better game.

Golf Digest, 1981

Making due allowances

Stephen Potter, who contributed hugely to the gaiety of nations by giving the world gamesmanship and one-upmanship, put his finger unerringly on the flaw in the system of golf handicaps.

Potter recognized that no matter how scientifically a man's handicap might be assessed, external factors having nothing at all to do with golf could influence the way he plays on any particular day.

The solution suggested by Potter was to convert a one-armed bandit into a handicap adjustment machine. You would feed pertinent information into the machine concerning the state of your health and morale, pull the lever and the machine would deliver your adjusted handicap for the day.

When *Golfmanship* was published the technology of computers was in its infancy but now, thanks to microchips, we have the gadgetry to pursue Potter's ideas to a sophisticated conclusion. All we need is a computer terminal in every golf club, linked in a national network, and we are in business.

Before going out to play golf you would simply tap out on the terminal keyboard the current facts about your life and in a trice you would receive a printout of your handicap for the day. The hardware for such a scheme is easily provided. As for the software, the analysis and judgment of the information, the greatest care must be taken in programming the computer.

We must obviously have a national debate on the whole subject and I shall start the ball rolling with a few suggestions. Let us start with an easy one.

Input: soggy patch in backyard turns out to be seepage from rich oil deposit.

Printout: subtract three strokes from handicap.

Most of the information supplied to the computer will need a more thorough examination and supplementary questions will have to be prepared. For example, 'Portrait of wife's mother revealed to be a Whistler.' On the face of it the computer would reply, 'Subtract two strokes', but it must be programmed to probe ruthlessly and ask: 'Is wife insistent that family keep portrait for sentimental reasons?' If your answer is 'Yes' then you might well get a response of 'Add one stroke to handicap' to cover the disappointment and expense of having to insure the damn thing.

Some items of information will require quite a close cross-examination. For instance: 'College dropout son who has been bumming around Europe on your stolen American Express card returns to bosom of family with new bride.' How do we assess that occurrence for handicap purposes? The computer must not hesitate to offend moral susceptibilities in its search for the truth of the matter. 'Unless bride is princess of currently stable monarchy or heiress to Greek shipping fortune (in which case ignore all other considerations and subtract four handicap strokes), state her age, weight, beauty on a scale of 1 to 10, number of children, education, parentage, whether she wears shoes, does she speak English, earning capacity, dexterity with knife and fork.'

Since life for most of us tends more towards personal disasters than to matters for great rejoicing, most of the adjustments will be in the form of additions to the handicap allowance. I suggest that an automatic one stroke be given for:

Traffic cop gives ticket on way to club.

Shoelace snaps in locker room.

Breakfast toast is burned.

When fellow member who is a qualified doctor greets your arrival at the club by saying, 'Boy, that must have been some party.' (If in fact you had not been to a party but had spent a quiet evening followed by a full nine hours of sleep, add three strokes to handicap.)

We may get into some slight dispute over the allotment of extra strokes for business mishaps, but I suggest one stroke for 'Partner

absconds with your wife,' two strokes for 'Partner absconds with all the company cash' and three strokes for 'Partner absconds with your golf clubs.'

Naturally, golfers would be on trust to report their affairs honestly to the computer, but that is nothing new in golf. It is, after all, a game based on trust, although it might be feasible to incorporate a lie-detecting system into the terminal just to be on the safe side.

If it worked, as I am sure it would, then possibly the PGA might take a look at the idea for professional golf. After all, why should a man's livelihood be at risk of the everyday annoyances that affect his prowess on the course? A rude waitress serving the breakfast eggs can cost a pro a stroke or two, and this system could introduce an element of justice in golf.

'Chance meeting with Jack Newton in motel bar' should be worth the subtraction of two strokes from the next day's round or, if Newton has happened to miss the cut and is in a festive mood, the award could be as high as four strokes. And there was a redhead in Greensboro who was notoriously responsible for inflating scores of good golfers into the 80s. That is another story but the day may come when her influence can be adjusted equitably.

Golf Digest, 1981

Some diabolical strokes ————

My attention has been drawn to a new method of stroke indexing and I must tell you that my attention, thus drawn, has been behaving like a horse being led into a blazing building. I knew I was in trouble as soon as I caught the acrid whiff of the sentence: 'The independent variables can be justified *a priori*, on heuristic grounds, and *a posteriori* on the basis of their explanatory capacity.'

The source of my terror is the journal *Applied Statistics* which has published a paper by I.G.O. Muircheartaigh and J. Sheil of University College, Galway. These learned worthies sought to settle once and for all the arguments in the bar of their golf club by devising a statistical formula for determining the order of difficulty of the 18 holes.

They took the scores of 575 players for five competitions, broke them down into handicap categories over or below 10, and analysed the wind speed and direction. Much as I would like to reproduce the full thesis I must deprive you of that treat because it is in the copyright of the Royal Statistical Society (which is welcome to it).

A statistical model based solely on five results, two handicap categories, wind speed and direction cannot begin to build a data base for measuring the statistical difficulty of a hole. Reluctant as I am to introduce an element of complexity into the elegant mathematics of the Galway researchers I do feel that they must address themselves to some of the other vital factors which affect the playing difficulty of a hole.

They have, for instance, overlooked what might be termed the 'Night-before parameters'. Once I had to play a match at Little Island and the previous evening in search of spiritual elevation the golf correspondent of the *Daily Mail* and I set off from our Cork hotel to attend (if memory serves aright) an exhibition of water colours of local flora. By chance our route led us by a bar kept by a cousin of my companion and we stepped in to permit him to pay his family respects. As I stood at the bar in my flasher mac, sipping a slim-line tonic, an outraged voice yelled: 'Jasuss! It's Ian Paisley!' That misunderstanding had a considerable effect on my play of Little Island, making the first hole virtually unplayable.

Temperature is another important factor. When a golfer is swaddled up in multiple layers of wool his prospects of making par at an uphill 440-yarder are seriously impaired. Everyone is familiar with the conjuror's trick of holding a length of rope at arm's length and then tying a knot in it with a deft flick of the wrist. Less familiar, but widespread among us back sufferers, is a similar phenomenon with the spinal cord whenever the temperature falls below about 46 degrees Fahrenheit.

What of rain, snow, hail and heavy conditions underfoot? Cannot these independent variables also be justified *a priori* on heuristic grounds? Of course they can. They turn par-fours into fives.

Murphy's Law is a rich source of statistical variables. At a guess I would say that a broken shoelace in the locker room adds at least four strokes to the par of the golf course. Then there are domestic tiffs at breakfast, punctures on the way to the club, variations in the FT index and arguments with the secretary.

They may be difficult to reduce to statistical terms but the task must be tackled because they do have a bearing on our ability on the course. Angry golfers tend to press and perform badly on holes with trouble down the left.

Finally we come to the most important factor of all. Never mind the weather or the conditions, nothing influences the way we play so much as the company we keep. Not even the most disciplined professionals are immune from the effects of this variable. Any mathematical formula which seeks to postulate how you and I are going to play the course, which is what the stroke index attempts, must take account of our playing companions.

It is no use simply identifying the fidgeters, the whistlers, the dawdlers, the rule-benders and the greyhounds and postulating that since they comprise 40 per cent of the membership then everyone will have an off day twice in every five monthly medals. This variable is further complicated by the fact that what gets up your nose may disturb me not at all.

The most potent example of this factor in my experience came from an unlikely source. I was drawn to play a match with a man I knew by reputation to be a model of behaviour on the course and I was looking forward to the game because, again from his reputation, I felt confident of beating him.

We introduced ourselves on the first tee, wished each other good luck and drove off. Hardly had we started walking down the fairway than he burst into song. Just a snatch, but fortissimo. 'There's a bright golden haze on the meadow. . . .' We walked a little further. 'On the road to Mandalay-ay.' I gave him a marked look. He appeared uneasy and responded with a nervous smile. A short burst of 'Old Man River' followed and moments later he launched into a faltering rendition of 'Give me cracked corn and I don't care.'

On this occasion he mistimed his entry by about a semi-breve and I had the first clue to the mystery. I monitored his musical outbursts and there was no doubt about it; the poor chap was suffering from a condition usually associated with horses. He was broken winded. When he walked it happened quite spontaneously about every 10 paces, except that he could not be sure that it might not be 12 paces, or 15.

His attempts to cover his, and my, embarrassment with song was futile from then on but he was in such agonies of self-consciousness about his temporary affliction that I thought it kindest, mistakenly on reflection, to pretend that I had not noticed. I was totally undone and found myself listening for his unscored grace notes. It is, as I can now assert with the force of a law of nature, impossible to play golf while waiting for your opponent to break wind. He won easily.

When statisticians come up with a formula which incorporates such independent variables I will look with a kinder eye on their work. My feeling is that any mathematical approach of stroke indexing is a function of match-play results only, since the index is a function of match-play. Better still, let us retain the traditional system of fixing the index by means of furious arguments in the bar.

The Observer, 1984

No two ways about it ────────

Those of us who start each day with a devotional reading from the good book, the Rules of Golf as authorised by the Royal and Ancient Golf Club of St Andrews, will be aware that deep in the Apocrypha a profound change has taken place.

In the chapter headed Appendix 11, known to golf scholars as St Frank's First Letter to the Philistines, or more simply as The Rigmarole, the word 'wood' has been replaced by the expression 'non-metallic club with a loft or face angle not exceeding 24 degrees'.

Now these appendices are not rules of golf, otherwise they would be included in the rules. They are detailed explanations, interpretations, guidance and suggestions, and the two which are specifically labelled 'rules' cover amateur status and are universally ignored.

In the case of Appendix 11, this is a scientific codification of a real rule, Rule 4, which states in the part that matters: 'The club shall not be substantially different from the traditional and customary form and make.' Apart from the unfortunate element of tautology, that rule is an admirable declaration of holy writ. It is clear and precise and it represents an expression of the main function of the ruling bodies, which is to act as guardians of the game's heritage. And one of the glories of that heritage is the wood.

What could be more traditional and customary in form and make than the wooden golf club? It is the one artefact of the game in which artistry triumphs over technology. The wooden club has been central to the golfing story since the earliest days. The best of the wooden clubs, from the long nosed, spliced baffies of pear wood to the polished persimmon of today's craftsmen, are revered as works of art, as functional sculpture.

Nearly every great achievement in the game, from Monsieur Samuel Messieux's record drive with a feathery ball in 1836 to Bobby

Jones' Grand Slam of 1930 and Gene Sarazen's killer albatross at the 1935 Masters, has been accomplished with the indispensable aid of wooden clubs. By what right have the authorities officially eliminated the wood from golf?

You are entitled at this point to stem the diatribe by raising your hand and suggesting that golf cannot live in the past. The game must keep up with the times. Progress must not be stifled by sentiment. Metal woods, if you will excuse the expression, are not a passing fad. They are here to stay. They are more durable and more effective and will inevitably supplant woods entirely in the years ahead. So what is so reprehensible about the ruling bodies facing facts?

Very well, let us continue the discussion under strictly current, high-tech terms of reference, leaving aside the issue of the gross dereliction of the ruling bodies' responsibilities as guardians of the game's heritage as embodied in Rule 4. Let us concede their right, which they undoubtedly possess, arbitrarily to render legal clubs illegal by inventing a new system of measuring grooves. Let us grant them the power to sweep away the distinctions between woods and irons which have been a fundamental part of golf for hundreds of years. Let us go along with the philosophy that anything new must be an improvement and should be allowed provided it falls within those decimalised parameters of Appendix 11.

In that case Rule 4 has to go. They cannot insist on traditional and customary form and make in the rules and encourage non-traditional and non-customary forms and makes in the appendices. We golfers have to accept enough anomalies as it is, such as moving balls being deemed to be stationary, and a ball sitting there in plain sight as being officially lost, but there is a limit.

Admittedly, wooden clubs have not been banned; only the word 'wood' has been expunged. And, indeed, special concessions over the dimensions of grooves for non-metallic clubs with loft angles less than 24 degrees have been retained in Appendix 11. But this itself raises an anomaly which has nothing to do with any sentimental attachment to the past. Take the case of the model of 'irons' whose heads are in fact constructed of carbon fibre. In the brave, new, scientific world of golf legislation, the grooves of the long irons can be wider and deeper than those of the mid and short irons.

Likewise, club-heads are required to be generally plain in shape, with all parts rigid, structural in nature and functional. That is clear enough; no decoration is permitted. When did you last see a club with no decoration?

My point, in case it has escaped you, is that the ruling bodies cannot have it both ways. Either equipment can be of traditional and customary form and make, a subjective judgment the members of the

Rules of Golf Committee are well qualified to make, or it can be defined in rigorous, scientific specification. Mixing the two concepts simply does not work.

Golf World, 1989

Remove the stigma

Is there disgrace in being disqualified? I share the view of many golfers that there must be a stigma attached to disqualification. It is, after all, golf's equivalent of the red card, of Eddie Waring's 'early bath' and of being plugged through the gizzard during a poker game in the Long Branch saloon in Dodge City.

If a golfer deliberately cheats he is disqualified. But the same punishment is suffered by a player who innocently and inadvertently commits a technical breach of rule. He is branded with the same mark.

One line of argument has it that it is the crime which carries the disgrace, not the punishment. Thus a Christian martyr who was burnt at the stake was ennobled rather than disgraced, while a multiple murderer who suffered the same fate was disgraced. The weakness of that thesis is that the martyr patently suffered a gross miscarriage of natural justice, but in golf there is no question of the rules being wrongly applied. We are not talking about players being wrongly disqualified; we are discussing the anomaly that the technical offender and the deliberate cheat are lumped together and treated equally by disqualification when the laws are scrupulously applied.

Bernard Gallacher failed to return his card in the Coral Classic and he was disqualified. He was upset. There is no player in European golf who is more meticulous in observing the rules, and in seeing that his fellow competitors are equally scrupulous, and it hurt him deeply to be disqualified under the same rule (38) which provides a similar punishment for marking your card with a 3 on a hole where you actually took 4. I cannot remember a tournament in which at least one competitor was not disqualified but disqualifications for cheating come along once in a blue moon. You can be disqualified for playing from outside the teeing ground, for using clubs with grooves .036 inches wide, for using an unapproved ball or even a specimen of an approved ball which happens not to conform to the official specifications although it is impossible for a golfer to measure the legality of his ball, for using a 15th club, for changing the playing characteristics of clubs or ball during play, for agreeing to waive a rule, for failing to hole out, for practising on the course on the day of a competition, for failing to refer a disputed decision to the committee immediately after the round, for playing in incorrect order in foursomes, for influencing the position or movement of the ball, for playing a wrong ball, for dropping incorrectly, for employing two caddies, for being late on the tee, for discontinuing play without satisfactory reason, for repeatedly delaying play, for denying another competitor's rights, for using an artificial device, for failing to sign the card, for returning a score lower than actually taken, for failing to lift your ball on the green when requested by a fellow competitor. And also, of course, for cheating, which means deliberately breaking any of the rules. That comes under Rule 1 although I defy anyone to justify such an interpretation from the obscure wording of the rule. I would much prefer to see the penalty of disqualification reserved for deliberate breaches of rule, committed with the intention of gaining an unfair advantage. Then the stigma of disqualification would be justified. However, there are numerous possibilities for innocent technical offences which result in the player not completing the stipulated round. Take the case of Tony Jacklin during the Open championship at Troon in 1973. He dropped clear of a rabbit hole and the ball rolled about a yard into a much more favourable position, although not nearer the hole. In a true spirit of sportsmanship, albeit in ignorance of the provisions of Rule 22–2c, he felt that this lucky bounce had given him an unfair advantage and so he dropped again.

He was penalised, and properly so, but the incident perfectly illustrated how easy it is to run foul of the rules of golf even when trying your damndest to abide by the letter and spirit of the game. He could just as easily have been disqualified while acting in the same spirit of fair play. It has happened to thousands of golfers.

What I would like to see is the legalisation of the ritual of tearing up your card. At the moment if a golfer fails to return a properly attested and signed card, for whatever reason, he is disqualified. It is sometimes recorded by the euphemism 'No return' but that is entirely unofficial, with no standing in the rules of golf. But how would it be if a player discovered that he had inadvertently committed a disqualification offence and he then had the option of tearing up his card and being officially posted as a no return? There could be no possible stigma attached to a no return.

I would go further and permit a player to tear up at any time, for any reason, provided that his withdrawal from the competition in no way inconvenienced his playing companions. At the present time a player has to resort to inventing a phoney injury if he wishes to withdraw, usually a pain in the back. But why should not a player withdraw if he is playing badly, or is fed up, or thinks he has no chance of winning a decent prize?

What about the spectators who have paid to watch? They would be narked if players walked off the course wholesale. But there would not be mass walk offs. The incentive to play on is powerful and the only golfers who would walk off are those, like Bob Charles in the English Classic at The Belfry, who are playing so badly that they are not worth watching for the time being. Charles felt that he was hindering his playing companions and by withdrawing he was doing them a service.

Let us reserve the sledgehammer of disqualification for the cheats and introduce the no return for the innocents who, for whatever reason, want out.

Golf Digest, 1989

Chapter 5

Home from home at the club

A tilt at windmills

On balance, last year was a bad, sad year for golf. The good things –
and 1979 had its moments – were overshadowed by the collapse of
the most imaginative and far-sighted reform in the history of the
game. I refer, of course, to the proposal by the recreational committee
of the North East Fife Regional Council to dig up the putting green of
the Old Course at St Andrews and to build a crazy golf course under
the windows of the Royal and Ancient club.

In a 'free society', decisions reached by democratic process can
always be reversed by those same processes, as enlightenment
breaks through the ignorance and prejudice of the elected representatives of the people, and so in theory we cannot say that this scheme
is lost for ever. But for the moment we have to accept that the plan is
doomed.

Nowhere will the disappointment be more keenly felt than within the
R and A. The excitement of the members at this proposal, with its
important social and economic implications, was evident on every side.

As I understand the position, the R and A was willing and anxious
to offer every assistance to the crazy golfers. An ad hoc advisory
committee was ready with a draft constitution for a Crazy Golf
Association after its first suggestion, that the R and A simply absorb
the army of crazy golfers and rename the club the Royal and Ancient
and Crazy Golf Club, had met with resistance from some of the
stuffier overseas members.

The idea was that Garrards be commissioned to produce a
perpetual trophy in the form of a stick of candy floss, created in silver,
to which the crazy golf champion should attach a replica, in silver, of
a bucket and spade.

The Rules of Golf committee had placed its massive resources at
the disposal of the crazy golfers and had actually started work on a
crazy golf code incorporating such provisions as Ball Jammed in
Clown's Mouth, Toffee Apple (Or Part There of) Adhering to Ball,
Ball in Motion Stopped or Deflected by Screaming Infant during
Temper Tantrum, and Stationary Ball Moved by Vane of Windmill
Kicked Off by Spotty Faced Hooligan.

Now, alas, all these progressive ideas must be suspended. What
might well be interpreted as a truce formula for the class war
remains unratified. Following the breakdown in negotiations to build
holiday chalets alongside the Road Hole, this is indeed a bitter set-
back to all men of liberal persuasion.

However, we must not be discouraged. There is comfort to be had in the very fact that the plan was mooted, defined and carried in committee. That shows a true awareness of the needs of the day. The men who wish to push back the frontiers of progress may have lost a battle but the war continues. There is much which can be done to improve the amenities of St Andrews as a holiday resort by putting the drab acres of the Old Course to more profitable use and thereby produce a valuable new source of revenue for the privy purse.

Out at the turn, for example, there is a triangle of land bordered by the eighth, eleventh and part of the seventh holes. It just sits there, with only an occasional visit from a very bad golfer. Why not put it to productive use? It would serve well as the site for a fairground amenity of the type which used to be called a helter-skelter but these days more often goes under a space age name such as a Canaveral Blast-off.

How would the day-trippers get there in safety? After all, it would be absurd to expect them to walk, risking life and limb from flying golf balls. From long acquaintance with the Old Course I do believe that it would be feasible to build a monorail up the middle of the course. Nearly every golfer who plays St Andrews remarks on the excessive size of those double greens and they would surely not object to the odd concrete stanchion. They would provide unusual hazards and add to the variety of the golf, in much the same way that the Old Course Hotel has enlivened this tired old pasture.

There are sure to be fuddy-duddies who say that it would be sacrilege to despoil the Old Course in this way. The golf would be ruined. Fie to such thoughts. What does it matter if your drive is impeded by a sand bunker or by an ice-cream stall? The challenge of the shot, calling for a cut-up nine-iron, for instance, remains unimpaired. Even enhanced. No true golfer would shirk from trying a delicate ricochet off a hamburger stand if it meant getting his ball close to the hole.

But where, you reactionaries ask, is your sense of history? This would be committing an obscenity in the cathedral of our noble game. Not at all. There is an excellent historical precedent for such embellishments of the Old Course. What student of golf does not know of the famous ginger beer cart which used to stand alongside the fourth hole and where the ginger beer, so tradition has it, was sometimes laced with brandy?

No, no. I insist that the recreational committee is on the right tracks in seeking ways to maximise the cost effectiveness of the Old Course and to spread the resort appeal of St Andrews right across the social spectrum. On the other hand, if anyone cares to collect those councillors who are intent on turning the Old Course into Coney Island and send them to Mars on a one-way ticket, then I do believe that such action would be an even better idea.

The Observer, 1980

Finding the best club

Some years ago, when my journalistic integrity was withering in the shadow of the bailiff, I was persuaded to compile a list of the 50 greatest courses outside America. In self-defence I must state that I put up token resistance to this idea, countering with an offer to list the parts of the body in order of their importance. The editor, making stabbing motions in the direction of my chest with the pen that signs the cheques, insisted that it must be courses. So be it.

A number of most unpleasant consequences followed publication of my list. Whenever I crossed the threshold of a club which had not been favoured by my imprimatur, I was roundly assailed as a cretinous charlatan. Even those clubs which did appear on the list were cool in their welcome, hurt by not being rated higher up the pecking order. Everywhere I went I ran into a palpable wall of suspicion that I had been heavily bribed (not true, alas).

The experience confirmed the impression that every club member believes his home course to be the best in the world, an undiscovered masterpiece. This self-deluding loyalty and devotion of the golf course of one's home club is a highly satisfactory state of affairs and I shall do nothing to challenge it. In any case, the listing of golf courses has grown into a major industry and can get on very well without my intervention.

But I detect a gap in the market of listings. Nobody, so far as I am aware, has attempted to list golf clubs. After all, a round of golf is a round of golf and for most of us that means a most dispiriting experience. All of us like to regard ourselves as rational human beings, well capable of conducting ourselves according to the dictates of common sense. And yet you have only to observe a pro-am to confirm my contention that golf brings the wisest and greatest of

116

men face-to-face with the irrefutable proof that they are useless.

That is not much fun. What makes golf such a wonderful game is that afterwards you go into the clubhouse, where scar tissue quickly forms over the self-inflicted wounds to your psyche. You brag about your one good shot of the day; you lie about your bad luck and claim that you were distracted on your bad shots. You get a big laugh from your latest joke. Pretty soon, under the soothing balm of the convivial atmosphere, your self-esteem is restored and you go home with a glow of satisfaction from a wonderful day's golf.

The club, rather than the course, is the major source of golf's pleasures. And the membership rather than the building and its amenities is what makes the club. The constituents which form the spirit of a golf club are difficult to analyse but an example may help. At Royal Portrush in Northern Ireland a member has converted his locker into a cocktail cabinet, generously supplied with a wide variety of nourishing restoratives. He leaves the key on top of the locker and every member is welcome to help himself as and when the spirit moves him.

You might imagine that this would be an expensive gesture. Plenty of members avail themselves of Sam's hospitality when reaching the safe refuge of the locker room after battling the elements which assail this great championship links. But, this being a good club, the practice quickly grew among the members of topping up the supplies of this welcome free bar. Every so often you quietly slip a bottle into Sam's locker and thus is perpetuated a highly civilised tradition.

If you want to test whether you belong to a good club, just ask yourself whether the system of Sam's locker would work at your club. Or would it be abused? Would it be tolerated by the board of management? Would the contents be pilfered by the staff? Would some snake among the membership inform the authorities that intoxicants were being dispensed without the benefit of a licence? Satisfy yourself on these points and you can take pride on belonging to a good club. If you determine that the entire membership is composed of Sams, then you belong to a very good club indeed.

Golf skill is irrelevant when it comes to assessing a good member. The important thing is to be clubable, which means rather more than just not being obnoxious. For starters we might say it means declining to join conspiracies to have the manager dismissed, or the greens reshaped; not making lewd references to the women members; keeping the volume of your conversation at a level which makes life tolerable for everyone else; standing your corner at the bar and delivering your due quota of witty stories.

You can no doubt revise or supplement these requirements. If you belong to a great club, then let me know the details of what makes it so good and we can start to compile the list of the greatest clubs in golf. To start the ball rolling, I would like to nominate Royal Portrush and Pine Valley in New Jersey as worthy candidates for the top-10.

Golf World, 1990

A little knowledge . . .

'Good gracious, Abercrombie, what are you doing here?'

'I am applying for the position that was advertised, sir.'

'But my dear fellow, this panel has been assembled to appoint a new chief surgeon to St Swithin's hospital.'

'That's right, sir.'

'I should explain, gentlemen, that this man is known to me. Angus Abercrombie is the Keeper of the Green at Green Meadows Golf Club where I have the honour to be Convenor of the Green Committee. May I ask, pray, whether you have any medical qualifications, Abercrombie?'

'None whatsoever, sir. Not formal, academic qualifications.'

'So you know nothing whatsoever about the human body?'

'I wouldn't say that, sir. After all, I've had one of my own all my life.'

'Yes, yes. Of course you know that everyone has one head, two arms and two legs, but that hardly qualifies you for the post of chief surgeon.'

'Well I was not proposing that I should do any of the manual work, all that cutting and stitching. I see the job of chief surgeon more as a supervisory role. You know the kind of thing, laying down a policy.'

'What policies do you have in mind to advance the science of surgery?'

'The first thing I would do is eliminate the left kidney. After all, we can all manage very nicely on the one.'

'So why did the Almighty provide us with two kidneys?'

'Just for the sake of symmetry, sir. They way I see it, the left kidney is the same as that bunker down the right side of the second, the one you had filled in because you kept slicing into it. If you recall, sir, you said that Alister Mackenzie only put it there for the sake of appearances.'

'And what other innovations do you have in mind?'

'I would give instructions that all post-operative patients must be made to drink 10 gallons of water a day. Get rid of all those poisons.'

'Ten gallons a day! Good lord, man, you'd have to give them all drains.'

'Not drains, sir. They are a complete waste of money, or so you always say.'

'That amount of fluid would cause all manner of complications.'

'Funny you should say that, sir. Those were the very words I used when we put in the automatic sprinkler system and you ordered me to give the greens a half-hour drench every night. I said that we would have complications, invasion by annual meadow grasses and fungus diseases, and you said we could treat those problems with chemicals. If the patients get the human equivalent of *poa annua* and fusarium we can give them antibiotics.'

'That would be a disastrous clinical practice, Abercrombie, and horrendously expensive.'

'Don't you worry about the money, sir. After all, it is not as if it is coming out of our pockets. Anyway, I've got some ideas for economies.'

'Such as?'

'Growths. You know at the club I keep on about clearing the underbrush from the woods to improve the ventilation, help natural evaporation and so stop excess water oozing down onto the fairways? And you keep saying to leave it the way it is and let nature take its course? Well, I would do the same at the hospital. Just think of the money we would save.'

'You realise no doubt, Abercrombie, that diet is tremendously important for good health. St Swithin's is fortunate in that we have our own hospital farm to produce the patients' meals. Strictly organic, of course. I take it that you would not wish to make any change in that arrangement. You have some bee in your bonnet about making compost and using nothing else to feed the greens on the golf course.'

'That's right, sir. Compost and sand is all I recommend because that's all the grass needs and it costs practically nothing. But you have shown me the error of my ways by insisting that we follow the regime that the salesman from the chemical company suggested to you the day when he gave you that radio telephone for your car. So I wouldn't bother with the farm produce for the hospital. I would put the catering out to tender to one of the fast-food chains.'

119

'Well, thank you, Abercrombie for giving us the benefit of your ideas. I am afraid that we are unable to offer you the post of chief surgeon but you have certainly given us something to think about.'

Golf World, 1990

Leave well alone

Golf club committees are great tinkerers. There may be some huffing and puffing at my selection of the word 'tinkering' because those who commit tinkering are always firmly convinced that the activity in which they are engaged is improving things.

And, of course, very often the result of tinkering is an improvement. However, it is still tinkering, and in all too many cases the tinkering by one chairman of the greens committee is restored by the man who succeeds him in office.

It might be an enlightening exercise for a senior member with time on his hands to research the history of tinkering, de-tinkering and re-tinkering at his club and produce a balance sheet documenting the sheer waste of money on the course over, say, the past 30 years.

In the course of a year I suppose that I visit nearly 100 golf clubs and inevitably I return to the same ones at regular intervals. I am always interested to observe the tinkering which has taken place since my previous visit and to try and detect the reason for the change.

It is no use asking the members because they are always wildly divided in their opinions, some castigating the change as the grossest folly, some championing a new bunker as a stroke of genius which has transformed a humdrum hole into the finest par-four in the land, and some incoherent with rage over the expenditure, regardless of the merits of the tinkering.

Objective discussion is further complicated by the fact that golf clubs tend to sub-divide into factions and the snooker room set will not hear a good word about the card room cabal, no matter what the objective merits of the tinkering might be.

The vast majority of golf clubs in the British Isles are outdated and

I am not referring to brown varnished lockers and eccentric plumbing in the clubhouse. As a matter of fact I rather like a whiff of the Boxer Rising in clubhouses, and deep leather armchairs with families of mice nesting in the recesses of horse hair, and ratty stewards who have been serving the members for 50 years and who grumble about only having one pair of hands.

That is après-golf and its quality depends much more on the club spirit of the members than on the age of fixtures and furnishings.

But the golf course is another matter. A golfer who pays for membership of a golf club is entitled, in my view, to the best golf which the site is capable of providing and it is all too rare to find a course which exploits its full potential.

Can we perhaps define what a golf course should be in this latter part of the 20th century? I would judge the quality of a course under three headings: Amenities, Condition, and Intrinsic Golfing Merit.

Amenities

A course, whether 9 holes or 18, should also have a practice putting green and a practice ground. Ideally, the member should be able to step from the locker room straight to the practice ground and have the facility to hit a bucket of balls. The balls should be provided (for a fee, naturally) by the pro. There is no greater waste of space at a golf club than a practice area where members take their own practice balls. It needs only one slashing gorilla to reduce five acres of open space to a no-go area.

Having loosened up with his bucket of balls, the golfer should now be able to progress in logical sequence to a putting green within sight and earshot of the first tee. He is now ready, in every sense of the word, when his tee time is called.

Condition

I regard it as scarcely less than a divine right for a golfer to play off grass tees, rather than mats, if it is humanly possible to maintain turf all the year round. He is also entitled to have closely mown fairways and good putting surfaces.

Mats and temporary greens are an abomination, doubly so when they are unnecessary. Of course, heavy clay courses present problems during the soggy winter months but these problems can be overcome. The cure starts with an efficient system of drainage, a dull subject and difficult to sell to the annual meeting, especially when

121

accompanied by an appeal for funds, but it is impossible to have a good course without it. A golf course is like a bathroom, in that all the fancy tiling in the world is pointless unless the plumbing is right. That means drainage and irrigation.

Under the heading of condition, we might have to consider rebuilding tees and greens, with proper substructures and surfaces, but we will come to that in a moment.

Intrinsic golfing merit

For myself, I see this subject of course layout as subservient to both amenity and condition. It is also the most contentious subject, since every member believes himself to be a natural-born course designer. However, if a club is sold on Amenity and Condition, then some rearrangement of the course design will almost certainly be needed. Outside professional help should be sought for in the long run it will be better, cheaper and more likely to meet the approval of the members if an architect prepares the plan.

That, you may say, is all very well but a total reorganisation of the course would cost thousands, much more than the club could afford. The argument is specious. Working to a master, 10-year plan the reorganisation of a course need cost no more than the wasteful tinkering which the club undertakes in the normal way. It comes down to tinkering in accordance to a long term plan, a plan which is revised as the years go by. But in the end the tinkering adds up to a worthy, modern golf course.

Golf World, 1986

Dressing the part

It was difficult to put a finger on the source of unusual satisfaction provided by the professional golf of the past few weeks. What could be the elusive quality which was so agreeable about such disparate events as the Ryder Cup match, the Dunhill Cup and Ken Brown's victory in the Southern Open at Columbus, Georgia?

Of course! The common denominator finally hit me: in each case the players wore proper trousers. For some time I have been troubled by the sight of our fairway heroes playing golf in what appeared to be pyjama bottoms as tailored for Mr Les Dawson and made of fabric more suitable for the Sunday morning religious observance of polishing the car.

You may surmise that I am an old fool (correct) who knows nothing of fashion (correct) and who is jealous of famous players being handsomely paid by clothing manufacturers to play in fancy dress (correct again).

You would be wrong to assume, however, that I care nothing for appearances and keeping up with the times. I do, I do. Dress is very important as a badge of tribal identity. Manners makyth man but clothing proclaims the man and, despite the difficulty of defining the tribe of golf writing, I go to considerable lengths to dress the part, setting aside one morning a year to visit my tailor.

Indeed, some time back I reluctantly had to end my long association with Millett when his supply of Second World War Australian army bush hats and ex-submariners' heavy duty oiled wool seaboot stockings, one careful owner, was finally exhausted.

There followed a brief hiatus, my scruffy period, and then while driving along Interstate 85 one day I observed a hoarding inviting me to take a short detour to the High and Mighty Factory Outlet Mall at High Point, North Carolina, which turned out to be a building not much larger than the Earls Court exhibition centre and fitted with several miles of clothes racks.

Fastidious as ever, I rejected some 98 per cent of the assembled merchandise with one slow panning movement of the head and made a beeline for the rack marked 'Special Offer, 50 per cent off'. They are terribly well organised in such places with separate racks for every permutation of width and length and within two minutes I had a year's supply of dress for every occasion and was back at the checkout desk enquiring if they supplied the tape which men use to stick up their bottoms.

As usual, there followed a brief exchange to clarify the nuances of our common language and the proprietor, or possibly head cutter, insisted that my bottoms would be expertly stitched and pressed and delivered to my hotel.

We fell to chatting and I enquired: 'Tell me, Outlet-Mall, your professional recommendation for golfing dress.' 'Golf,' he replied, 'is an old and respectable game of long established tradition and these things should be reflected in the golfer's appearance combined, of course, with freedom in the regions of shoulders and the crotch.'

'My feelings exactly,' I replied.

My annual visits involve serious inconvenience, since perforce I have to justify them by covering the Greater Greensboro Open, than which professional golf offers no more trying experience, but I suffer it for the sake of continuing my association with a tailor of Outlet-Mall's perception.

His prescription for golf dress might well have been based on my earliest model, Frank Boultard, the professional at West Kent in the days when I was young and impressionable. Frank invariably wore a well pressed tweed suit of plus-fours, collar and tie, of course, and brown leather shoes which shone with a lustre which would have done credit to a sergeant-major.

In a way, Frank was a sergeant-major himself for in those days professional golfers saw themselves to be the non-commissioned officers of the game, highly trained experts and custodians of regimental standards who would never dream of setting foot in the officers' mess unless invited.

Frank liked it that way but he was one of the last of the breed in a world of social change. As professional golf established itself as a regular spectator sport so the dress of the players progressed with the times, with Henry Cotton showing the way and young players such as Peter Alliss and Arnold Palmer taking over in due course as role models for the game.

Some, like Neil Coles, remained faithful to the conservative greys and tans while others took their colourful lead from Jimmy Demaret and Doug Sanders but, regardless of individual taste, the universal rule was for golf dress to be casual-smart.

Latterly there has been an unfortunate lapse into dress which might be described as casual-scruffy, with more than a hint of shapeless discoland, on the golf course. I blame that Bob Geldof, admirable though he may be so long as you do not have to look at or listen to him.

The scandalised culprits of this trendy tat may well ask if I know how much they have to pay for their gear. That is beside the point: a crease is a crease is a crease which no designer label can excuse so far as I am concerned. If anyone wishes to wear clothes which look as if they had been made for someone else and slept in for a week then I would be the last person to criticise him as he departs for his evening's entertainment.

But on the golf course a player is on duty and he should be setting an example for the rest of us to follow. Heaven knows, some of us need all the good examples we can get.

The Observer, 1987

Trip the light fantastic

My editor is a tough journalist of the old school, with a Dick Tracey jawline and a tendency to bark, 'Get to the point, damn it! Sock it to 'em in the first paragraph. None of your effete, discursive ramblings – jump right into the subject.' Fearful of his wrath, I hereby declare that this column is about sugar, Mount Everest, golf cars, retirement villages, hamburger joints and feet. Specifically feet. Your feet and my feet.

There! Now may I please get back to my effete, discursive ramblings? I had pulled off Interstate 405 for lunch and reflected for the 100th time how Americans took hamburger joints for granted. Good, cheap food in clean surroundings is part of the national heritage.

Afterwards I had to make a detour on a one-way system and, being absorbed in my contemplative mood, missed the turn and finally wound up in a retirement village. It seemed to go on forever, acres of trim villas with, in most cases, golf cars parked in the drives.

In such a quiet residential area a golf car is an eminently suitable vehicle to drive to the supermarket and even to the golf club but, as witness the vast bags of ironmongery strapped to the cars, most of them were obviously used on the course. Shock! Horror! Could this be a commune of dissidents, defiantly holding out against *Golf Digest*'s enlightenment campaign to get golfers walking again? No, they were just retired people who preferred to ride.

Who can blame them? Recently I have slowed down myself, I realized. Pressing previous engagements prevent me from accepting 36-hole invitations, which did not happen 10 years ago. In those days there was no previous engagement so pressing that it could not be switched – or cancelled or forgotten if there was a chance for a full day's golf.

Lately, when early dusk requires that the lunchtime conviviality in the bar be cut short if 18 holes are be be completed, I sometimes settle for another belt or two and a quiet 12 holes. When I do go the distance the 17th and 18th seem longer than I remember them of old.

After that experience in the retirement village, and with the subject of advancing years taking on a certain edge in my mind, I broached the question of physical energy preservation in the bar, golf clubs being wonderful places for serious research. The nearest thing to practical advice was a suggestion by a doctor to eat a chocolate bar at the halfway point. 'Sugar gives you energy, you know.'

Deep research into the chocolate-bar theory demonstrated it to be a complete myth. Sugar is fuel but it does not rev up the horse-power. That confirmed my prejudice, for I have always regarded sweet foods as tasty poisons. Sugar is a composite of carbon, hydrogen and oxygen, but I take it only after it has been detoxified through a rather complex chemical process in which natural sugar, as in grapes for instance, is trampled by barefoot peasants.

Then, by the kind of diligent persistence that wins Pulitzer Prizes, I unearthed a piece of research conducted on behalf of the team that first climbed Mount Everest. The object was to discover how much weight the expedition could carry, and how far, and how best to carry it. One surprising finding, which vitally affected the team's equipment, was that a man could carry seven times as much weight on his back or shoulders as on his feet for the same degree of fatigue. Could this vital fact help conquer the Everest of old age?

I hurried to weigh my golf shoes. They came out at nearly 4 pounds the pair, including a total of 10 ounces of mud. Get out your calculators and check the implications of these figures. In short, if I simply walk around the course in my golf shoes it is more tiring than if I wear shoes of half that weight and play a full 18 holes, carrying 11 pounds of bag and clubs on my back. And it works. Experiments among seniors have proved that you can push back the clock by switching to light shoes. Pensioners who have changed to light-weight shoes are tripping around golf courses like two-year-olds and scoring better, for fatigue affects concentration as well as the purely physical functioning of the body.

So my message to those retired folk off Interstate 405, and everywhere else, is to get light shoes, climb out of those golf cars and walk, with six or seven clubs slung across the shoulders in a light bag. That way you will push the clock back even further.

Golf Digest, 1986

Clear the way for golf

Golf is supposed to be a pastime which promotes good health and good fellowship and the playing of it should be a source of pleasure, satisfaction and unalloyed joy.

It does not always work out exactly according to that ideal. Indeed, among my circle of golfing friends, the salty language of frustration and dismay during the average four-ball reaches a pitch of intensity which has been equalled only once in my previous experience, and that was when a steam line burst in the engine room of HMS *Renown*.

However, unlike the stokers on that memorable occasion, the golfers are always anxious to return to their beloved torture chamber of a golf course so, on balance, there must be more gold than dross in the alloy of their joy.

One circumstance brings the golfer's morale to a point so low on the scale of misery that it surely has no place in a game designed for enjoyment. I refer to the lost ball, specially when it occurs in a place where a ball has no reasonable right to become lost.

Most of us can accept with a certain stoicism the disappointment of failing to carry a water hazard and watching the ball plunge into the irretrievable depths. That is a fair cop and a lost ball is no less than due punishment for our ineptitude.

But when a ball is lost as it just dribbles off the fairway, or unluckily drifts into trees, then a man is entitled to feel aggrieved. There is no pleasure in looking for golf balls, either for the victim or his companions or the people behind who may well be held up until the imperatives of the game's etiquette switch the signals to green.

I have no time for the John Knox philosophy of righteous retribution which says: 'You hit the ball into the rough, it is nobody's fault but your own if the ball is lost.' That attitude completely ignores the basic purpose of golf. It also denies what I hold to be a vital principle of golf, and of life itself, come to that, namely that the punishment should fit the crime.

Now we all know from experience that nine times out of ten a bad shot carries its own punishment. Top your drive 150 yards down the fairway and you have dished your chances of reaching the green in two shots, even if you have a perfect lie. If your ball finds a pot bunker from such a shot then the punishment is unnecessarily draconian. To lose a ball off such a shot is a mockery of the purpose of golf.

There are many ways of defining what a golf course ought to be, but I would like to assert that the specification should include a clause to the effect that a golf course is a place where it is virtually impossible to lose a golf ball (always excepting water hazards of course, which are one of the glories of the game). At this point I must stress that I am not advocating that golf courses should be made easier, not by so much as a single stroke. My purpose is to increase the pleasure of golf without diminishing the challenge.

Rough, even semi-rough, is a prime area for lost balls. Show me a hole which is dependent on rough for its defences and I will show you a bad hole. More often than not, when you hit into heavy rough you spend an age looking for the ball and when/if you find the thing your only recourse is to hack it via the shortest route back on to the fairway.

That is a suitable enough punishment for your crime. But we can achieve exactly the same result, with no time-wasting or lost balls, by cutting down the rough and blocking the route to the green with one, two or a hundred trees. At the same time we greatly enhance the appearance of the hole. (Links courses which cannot support trees can achieve the same results by contouring the areas bordering fairways with humps and hollows which can be trimmed to length which makes the loss of a ball unlikely.)

Semi-rough can serve a useful strategic purpose but it should be maintained at a length which makes the position of the ball easily visible, say twice the length of fairway grass.

Woodland, which may well greatly increase in my ideal golfing world, is the other major cause of lost balls. The trees themselves are not the problem but the underbrush. There is a place in the natural scheme of things for shrubs and bushes but so far as golf courses are concerned that place is behind teeing grounds and in areas where golf balls are unlikely to fall. The suitable ones should be carefully transplanted to sites where they can be enjoyed and serve the purposes of ecology and the rest should be torn out by the roots. Woodland should be clear and uncluttered underfoot, easily maintained with proper equipment, for as deep into the woods as a ball is likely to penetrate.

If this policy is pursued we should now have a golf course which does not claim a vast toll of lost golf balls and, with sensible husbandry, we can reduce the cost of maintaining the course.

Most greenkeepers and their club committees regard the cutting of greens and fairways as an end in itself, the sole purpose being to produce short grass. My view is that mowing should also be seen as the harvesting of a valuable crop.

Instead of leaving swathes of mown grass on the rough and semi-rough, greatly increasing the probability of lost balls and stifling new growth, the mowings can be collected by switching to suitable machinery and recycled. The same goes for the natural debris cleared from woodland. Turn those mowings and fallen leaves and weeds into compost and you have a better fertiliser than anything you can buy in the way of inorganic chemical compounds.

Thus, with planning, imagination and a fundamental review of attitudes about what golf ought to be, the course can be improved, the quality of play can be improved, and both club and members can save themselves money. Isn't that what we all want?

The Observer, 1984

Dressing to kill

A British golfer will not win the Open. I am sorry about that for we have a few potential champions around and a British victory would do wonders for the game. However, it is impossible.

Shallow minded critics have complained for years that British golfers are lazy, unambitious and unwilling to make the sacrifices which are necessary to pluck the game's richest plums. I have always felt that such arguments were specious, although I could not put my finger on the real reason for overseas domination of our championship.

Finally I have discovered the underlying cause of British failure and I have been kicking myself unmercifully for my blindness.

Now, after full research and acute observations, I am able to state categorically that it has been impossible for a British player to win the Open since 1967. (Hairsplitting pedants may demur at this assertion and point out that Tony Jacklin won the Open in 1969. So he did, but if you will bear with me a little longer you will realise that Jacklin's victory was actually an American triumph. We have to go back to Max Faulkner's win in the 1951 Open to find the last true roast-beef-and-Yorkshire-pudding British Open champion.)

The blinding flash of revelation which laid bare the secret of overseas domination in recent Opens came to me at the Dunlop Masters when Jose-Maria Canizares covered the front nine of the Duke's course at Woburn in 29 strokes. Naturally, that performance recalled his remarkable feat of bagging 11 birdies and an eagle in unbroken succession during the Swiss Open at Crans-sur-Sierre.

From there my train of thought naturally turned to Baldovino Dassu's score of 60 in the Swiss Open. The scene came back to me in vivid detail, with Dassu picking his ball out of the cup at the end of that historic round. As he bent down his fashionable trousers split asunder. That was it! I rushed to my reference books and checked the list of recent Open winners. Player, Jacklin, Nicklaus, Trevino, Weiskopf, Watson, Miller, Ballesteros. Different shapes, different sizes, different nationalities – but they had one common denominator: all of them wore quite remarkably tight trousers!

Now think about the British players who might have won those championships judged purely on talent. John Panton, Neil Coles, Christy O'Connor, Bernard Hunt ... gifted players, experienced players but in the trousering department ... ?

The effect of tight trousers is virtually to cut off blood supplies below the waist and that in turn means that the upper body gets double the usual ration of red corpuscles, oxygen, hormones, adrenalin and upper cylinder lubricant. The nervous system, with only half its usual territory to cover, is twice as effective, making the hands double sensitive and the brain doubly active. How can British golfers hope to compete against such supercharged players? Faulkner did it quite by accident because he wore plus-fours and therefore had to wear tight bindings, or garters below the knees to keep his stockings up. Jacklin, as you will recall, was a regular competitor on the American Tour at the time of his victory at Lytham and so his wardrobe was American.

My findings throw considerable illumination on the history of competitive golf. Harry Vardon (six Opens) wore plus-fours. So did Bobby Locke (four Opens). Locke never wore plus-fours again after his victory at St Andrews in 1957. That was a private gesture of grateful tribute to the enlightened action of the championship committee in waiving any penalty for the technical offence of failing to replace his ball on the precise spot on the last green but, significantly, once he took to wearing baggy trousers and his heart had to handle all the wasteful effort of pumping supplies right down to his toes and back again he never won another championship.

Walter Hagen, who was rather a vain man over his appearance, wore his belt very tight in order to present his athletic figure to best advantage. Come to think of it, Peter Thomson also had an hourglass figure on the course and he must have pulled his belt in a notch or two. Arnold Palmer is a bit of a mystery because he won a few championships and his trousers were in constant danger of falling down. He was forever hitching them up and the only explanation I can offer for his success is that he must have worn very tight underpants. I must ask him about that some day.

We have our tradition of fine tailoring in Britain, with standards of fit and comfort laid down by the high priests of Savile Row. Surely we cannot sacrifice all that for the sake of boasting a home grown Open champion? For mark my words, if once our British sporting heroes switch to tight trousers then the manufacturers will jump on the bandwagon and tight trousers will be all there is to buy in the shops. For myself I am not prepared to endure the discomfort which is why I am wary of that Nick Faldo. He is showing a distressing tendency to flout our baggy traditions and is compressing his extremeties into some fancy nether integuments these days. If he wins at Sandwich I shall switch to a kilt.

Golf World, 1984

Near fatal vision

I
FYOU
CANREAD
THESEWORDS
withoutanyformofoptical

aid then I earnestly entreat you to turn the page and seek other diversions, for today's text is taken from the sight-reading chart of your local optometrist.

My interest in this subject was aroused many years ago when Jack Nicklaus kindly arranged for three colleagues and myself to play Frenchman's Creek in Florida.

Owing to the natural process of physical degradation that attends man's journey into the sere and yellow years, I had recently been equipped with a pair of bifocals. Sighting through the top halves of the lenses I could distinctly identify the four-inch lettering of the word GENTS painted on a door at 20 paces, thereby eliminating those incidents of acute embarrassment in my days of uncorrected vision.

Golf presented a problem. Standing with the erect posture advocated by Ben Hogan, my line of sight passed through the lower lenses and the ball appeared as a furry white blob the size of an aspirin. Worse was to come. By holding my gaze on this curious object and pushing the glasses up onto my forehead, I could see the aspirin move its position by a good 2 inches, seemingly jumping clear of the path of the approaching club-head.

By bending forward and lowering my head until my chin was jammed firmly against my sternum, as if peering respectfully into the grave of a departed friend, I could see the aspirin rather more clearly but, as you can well imagine, the axis of my classical swing was thrown right out of kilter.

A crisis point was reached on that occasion at Frenchman's Creek when I missed the aspirin altogether. When they had tired of their crude and cruel charade of rolling about on the fairway in paroxysms of vulgar mirth, my companions reached a consensus: My club-head had passed over the ball by 11 inches.

Something clearly had to be done. The next time I went for an eye test I asked the oculist whether it was possible to make a pair of glasses with angled lenses, which would present the ball in clear focus at address and indicate the exact location of the ball and not give me a phantom image closer to my feet. The oculist, a mature lady of Oriental origin, answered inscrutably: 'Natural vision is always best.'

I gave her natural vision theory a test on the day following the club's annual dinner, an event traditionally devoted more to sluicing than browsing. A chill breeze striking eyes unprotected by their accustomed windscreen made them water copiously. The ball appeared as a parody of the Olympic symbol, a series of fuzzy, overlapping spheres. I swung at the pink one. The club-head buried in the turf 6 inches behind the cluster.

Then the other day I was walking through a street market and came upon a stall selling glasses. They had a tabloid newspaper of the lurid variety as a test card. You tried different glasses until you found a pair that suited you, noted its strength as indicated by a number and then chose your preferred style. I dropped the paper onto the road and started testing the wares. Suddenly there it was in sharp focus: 'Vicar in sex romp with choirgirl'. Not just the headline, mind you. I could read the body type clearly although the content was not to my taste, you understand.

I selected a style of half-moon glasses, so that I could see over the top of them up the fairway. What a revelation it was when I put down a golf ball. It looked enormous and every dimple stood out in sharp detail. I could even read the name of my favourite brand under its XXXXX. It is, I have to confess, taking me some time to adjust to the novelty of being able to see the object that I am attempting to strike, but I do believe that my research is on the right lines. I shall be most interested to hear from any specialists in this field to confirm that a new dawn may indeed be breaking for the legion of bespectacled golfers.

Golf Digest, 1990

An exceptionally heavy post bag followed publication of the above, from opticians, oculists, ophthalmologists and optometrists, a distressingly high proportion of them regaling me with variations of the original double-vision joke (attributed to Galileo, c. 1629) about the man who looked down, saw two, put the big one away on the grounds that it couldn't be his, and wet his pants. Ho, ho. But they also gave solid advice and information about special prescription glasses for golf, which enable you to focus clearly on the ball without image-jump, see distant objects and read your score cards. What is more, they can be made in special water-repellent glass or plastic so you can play in the rain without continually wiping the lenses. Consult your friendly optician.

Chapter 6

These blessed plots

The finest course of all ————

The late Bernard Darwin, the father of golf journalism and, indeed, the pioneer along with Neville Cardus of literacy on the sports pages, was a considerable player as well as a fine essayist. When he sailed to America to cover the inaugural Walker Cup match the captain fell ill and the man from *The Times* was co-opted to play and take over the duties of leading the side.

It was from Darwin that British golfers first learnt about Pine Valley. The course already had a fearsome local reputation by the time Darwin was taken there on a private visit in the twenties.

He played the first seven holes in level fours and then came comprehensively to grief at the eighth. He picked up his ball and, sad to relate, retired to the clubhouse after delivering judgment: 'It is all very well to punish a bad stroke, but the right of eternal punishment should be reserved for a higher tribunal than a green committee.'

So far as the outside world was concerned that peppery diatribe set the tone for all subsequent writing about Pine Valley. The course had its label and there was no shortage of lurid anecdote to fuel that myth.

The members relished these horror stories and took pride in Pine Valley's growing notoriety as the most penal, the most difficult and the most malicious course in the world. They offered bets that visitors could not break 100 at the first attempt, or beat the par 18-up with the benefit of five strokes a hole.

So my brain was thoroughly washed by doom and despondency before I set out for the backwoods of New Jersey to tilt my feeble lance at the gorgon of golf. A friend sped me on the way with the words: 'It is all very well for golfers of Walker Cup calibre but for the likes of you and I it is simply unplayable.'

As to that, and to all the rest of the weeping and wailing and spitting of blood about Pine Valley, I am now ready to respond with a cheery cry of 'Rubbish!' True, it demands a standard of accuracy which is beyond most golfers, myself near the top of the list. Equally true it exacts a scale of punishment which is positively Old Testament in its severity, six strokes being a common sanction for missing a fairway or one of the greens which rise like islands in a sea of unraked sand.

As for the bunkers, there is one turf-walled brute at the front of the short tenth whose name is prudishly rendered in official publications as the Devil's Advocate or the Devil's Pit or, getting closer to the truth of the matter, the Devil's ah, Aperture, or just DAH. It is about 8 feet in diameter and the same depth, with steps set into the sand to assist the exhausted and disgruntled golfer to get back to the surface at the end of his shift.

One player, accomplished enough to have scored 35 on the first nine holes, found this bunker off the tee and took 23 for the hole. Devilish intervention caused one four ball to run up an aggregate of 88 strokes at the 10th and another player, having ruined his card and his disposition by taking seven strokes to extricate his ball from the pit, sat on its rim with his feet dangling into the abyss and howled like a baby.

My favourite Pine Valley story is of the four ball which lost one of its members in the woods. Three of them sliced into the trees and the fourth hooked his ball wildly. After playing back into the open country the three slicers crossed the fairway to help their companion's search. They found his ball but he was nowhere to be seen.

The police delivered him back to the clubhouse late at night, somewhat the worse for drink. He had lost his bearings and wandered for miles through the forest and had celebrated his eventual contact with civilisation in the time honoured tradition of *après* golf.

All these tales – and everyone who has enjoyed the privilege of playing Pine Valley has a personal disaster to relate – bear out the horrific reputation of the course. But they tell only the lesser half of the story. Because of the perils which beset the golfer on every side, the charge of exhilaration he receives when he successfully carries his drive over 170 yards of sandy waste is proportionately increased.

The hitting of a green, a routine enough experience at your home club, becomes a thrill. As for holing across those undulating greens with surfaces as slick as polished marble, watching the ball swing as much as 20 feet on its roller-coaster route, the afterglow of achievement lasts for weeks.

So, while playing Pine Valley can be a penance, and nearly always is somewhere during the round, the agonies are the price which must be paid for the ecstasies. Provided you leave your ego back in the locker room, Pine Valley is a delight. The scenery alone is intoxicating and enhanced by the wildlife of what is in effect a 650-acre nature reserve.

When my friend asks what I scored, he will doubtless say: 'I told you that you could never get around it.' In terms of numbers that is a just comment but numbers, far from being the be all and end all of golf, are the least part of the game.

After Pine Valley, by a long way the finest course I have experienced, other courses will seem humdrum so I may very likely

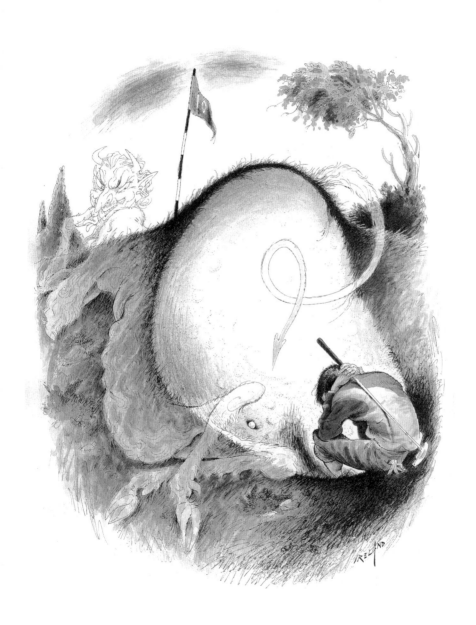

retire, to take up pursuits more suited to my creaking bones. It would be a pity to end on a high score but fitting to go out on the highest note of them all.

The Observer, 1985

A jewel in Sardinia

In Italy golf is not for the riff-raff. The game is the preserve of wealth and breeding and privilege. Walk through the locker room of any Italian club and you will stumble over the highly polished, hand-made shoes of dukes, counts and marquises, many of whom can trace their noble lineages back 20 and even 30 years to the day they bought their titles. They do themselves well, these Italian golfers, specially in the luxury of their clubhouses and the scope of the dining facilities. Fifteen years later I still get a touch of dyspepsia at the memory of a lunch in Garlenda golf club, near Alassio. One gets the impression that the course is an amenity, like the sauna or heated indoor pool, where the members can walk off the excesses of the mid-day meal and work up an appetite for the really serious business of the day, dinner.

It was therefore with some trepidation that I booked my flight from Rome to Sardinia, the trepidation somewhat increased by the (justified) fear that my luggage would go to Milan. After all, the hogsheads of champagne which had been pumped into the hog-heads of gossip writers from the gutter press had brought the publicists rich returns in the form of eulogies about the Costa Smeralda as the new jet set playground. St Tropez was passé; the in-place for the smart and wealthy was Pevero, whose crowning jewel was the golf club. Everyone, but everyone, from the Aga Khan (who developed the place) downwards was going there.

I approached with due irreverence, ready to curl my plebeian lip at the excesses of the idle rich. Admittedly it was slightly out of season at the time, but I was pleasantly surprised. There was no sign of Gunther Sachs; no topless Brigitte Bardot on the sands (a bit of a disappointment that) and no famous pop star in dark glasses pretending not to be wanting to be recognised.

The golf club was equally a surprise, in that the clubhouse was unpretentious and the course was clearly intended for serious golf. This was no place for a quiet stroll after lunch, but a challenge to intimidate a golfing tiger. Two golf architects had been brought in to create the course. Each, in turn, had cast an expert eye over the forbidding terrain and pronounced the job impossible. The third choice, the American Robert Trent Jones, came and cast an expert eye over the budget appropriation and pronounced: 'Sure, I'll build a course here.'

He certainly had a job on his hands. Sardinia was created by nature for *banditi*, a fugitive's paradise. Step 2 yards off the road, crouch down and a posse of 1000 policemen could never find you. The landscape consists of small, precipitous hills, strewn with boulders and covered with a lush vegetation of hardy shrubs and bushes. It is maquis country. Trent Jones planned to dynamite and bulldoze his way through, following the valleys and filling the ravines with rock to create level(ish) stretches for his fairways. He does not pussyfoot around, our Mr Jones. Since there was no topsoil he would ship it in by the boatload for the seed beds. Then, as he told me later, he noticed a peculiarity about the barren, Sardinian rock. When crushed it was not barren at all. 'Forget the boatloads of topsoil,' he ordered. 'Bring me a rock crusher.' Instead of carting rocks off the site he ground them down and spread the fine aggregate on the fairways, added grass seed and water and watched the lush greenery appear. That stratagem saved half a million dollars. Even so it was an expensive process and so today Pevero presents the golfer with a chilling ultimatum: Put your ball on the fairway or kiss it goodbye. Hit one off line here and the ball pongs off a boulder into the maquis to be lost forever. On occasion an intrepid golfer will venture into the scrub and find the ball but it is rarely worth it. You will break either your club or your heart attempting a recovery.

When golfers play Trent Jones courses they often get the idea that he is a malicious ogre with a grudge against anyone who takes a club in hand. In real life he is a mild, kindly man and his purpose is to reward good golf. It has to be really good, mind. The wayward golfer gets little joy from a Trent Jones course, but if you plan and execute a great stroke then you can feel an exquisite satisfaction not available on humdrum courses.

This potential for richly satisfying golf is enhanced at Pevero (and also the capacity for misery) by the brisk sea breezes which are seldom absent. For myself, I would not want to be condemned to play all my golf at Pevero but it is an exhilarating experience once in a while to be stretched to the limit, to tingle with white-knuckled, jaw-clenching, gut-wrenching anticipation on every shot. Death or glory every time you take out a club, even the putter because Trent Jones does not build billiard table greens.

When the Italian Open was held at Pevero a field of 50 professionals in the curtain-raising pro-am lost 81 balls between them. In one round an experienced tournament pro ran out of golf balls and had to go wading into an ornamental lake retrieving balls with his toes before he could continue play. It is a big, two-fisted, macho golf course off the back tees so there can be no question of patting it round with safe irons off the tee. You have to go for broke and there is no respite, no soft options to give you a breather on the way. Even if you play 17 holes well and step onto the last tee with the smug feeling that you can shut up shop and protect your score with quiet conservative golf, then Pevero still has shocks in store. The last hole is 617 yards, uphill, tight and treacherous. Good players run up sevens and eights without hitting what one would normally consider a destructive shot. The clubhouse, when you eventually reach it, looms like a sanctuary.

Maybe it is the lure of the breathtaking sea views from the clifftops which appear from time to time, or maybe it is the restorative power of Chianti, or possibly the sheer perversity of human nature, but next day, oddly enough, you cannot wait to get out there and have another crack at what must be the toughest golf course in Europe.

Homes Abroad, 1980

Augusta is not so tough

There cannot be a golfer alive who does not know what the Augusta National course looks like so this year I thought I might refrain from drivelling on about the azaleas and concentrate on the tactics for playing the course.

Who better to enlist for expert help in this matter than the players themselves, since the Masters field has represented the cream of world golf since 1934.

The first hole measures 400 yards, a drive and flick for the mighty hitters such as Frank Stranahan. Let us see how he played it in 1952.

Drive into the trees followed by some more embarrassing banging about for a seven. Oh dear. Never mind, these are the finest players of the modern era and they can easily recover from a shaky start. Step forward Sam Byrd and see if you can get a birdie or an eagle at the 555 yard second. The year is 1948 and his score tots up to 10.

The third is 360 yards long and in 1980 Douglas Clarke played it in eight strokes. Admittedly it is a tricky green. The fourth is a tough par-three of 205 yards and in 1965 Dave Eichelberger, on the eve of a distinguished professional career, took seven.

At 435 yards, the fifth is a demanding hole, with a narrow fairway by Augusta standards and a roller-coaster green. In 1965 the Little Master, Jerry Barber, took eight strokes. He later made a reputation as the designer of clubs with which it is impossible to shank.

The sixth is steeply downhill and plays much shorter than its nominal 180 yards. No score higher than a six has ever been recorded here in the Masters. Clearly the hole is a doddle and needs tightening up to give it interest. The perpetrators of those triple bogeys are legion, far too many to single out one individual as the exemplar of how to play the hole.

The seventh is a tricky driving hole because trees impinge and make half the fairway into inhospitable territory and in 1972 De Witt Weaver fell foul of those trees and took eight, giving him an average of 45 yards progress per stroke.

The eighth is a monstrous 535 yards, all uphill with the land on the left falling away into a wooded ravine. If you hook your ball down there, you can easily run up a score in double figures. Frank Walsh did just that in 1935, taking 12 to be precise.

And so to the turn and the switchback ninth of 435 yards. It is difficult to see how anyone could get into severe trouble on this hole but in 1948 Jack Selby managed it, taking eight and giving our team of selected experts an outward 74.

Let us nominate a big-hitter for the 10th, a par-four, even at 485 yards. Craig Wood once drove into the Spectacles bunker at St Andrews so he is a likely candidate to tame this mighty hole. His score in 1954 was eight.

The 11th is 30 yards shorter but more treacherous because this is the start of the infamous Amen Corner with Rae's Creek winding like a serpent across the landscape. In 1952, Dow Finsterwald made a significant contribution to the legend of Amen Corner with a nine on this one.

Nothing like that could ever happen at the 12th because the hole measures a mere 155 yards. You would back your grandmother to do better than nine on this hole, patting the ball along with her brolly. She would have to negotiate a humped-back bridge but she could make it. With his classic swing Tom Weiskopf was able to fly the ball through the air right up to the flagstick and this he very nearly did in 1980, the ball only being prevented from reaching dry land by an inconsiderate puff of wind.

Weiskopf walked forward to a point from which a player of his calibre could guarantee to pitch dead to the flag, dropped a ball and hit a delicately judged shot into the water. With a calm which belied his reputation for pyrotechnics, he held out his hand and his caddy placed in it another ball. Weiskopf dropped it over his shoulder in what was then the approved manner, swung his club with the lazy tempo of a man in perfect control of himself and his game and pitched the ball into the creek. And so it went on, and on, and on until, eventually, he got a ball to stop on the green and putted out for 13. His average for that hole was 11.92 yards for each stroke.

The 13th, a short par-five at 465 yards, calls for manipulation rather than muscle so who better than a dextrous Oriental to demonstrate how to play it. Observe Tsuneyuki Nakajima in 1978. Hang on, he is short with his approach shot and his ball is down among the water moccasins in the creek. He leaves it in there with his first recovery attempt and decides to change clubs. The caddy drops his new selection and it hits the ball. Nakajima is growing noticeably more scrutable by the minute. The only sound in the crowd is the clicking of his manager's abacus: drive, wedge, spoon, wedge, sand iron, wedge, plus penalty strokes just like VAT, and the total comes to 13.

The 14th, at 405 yards, has little potential for drama and it takes a real Augusta specialist, former Amateur champion Charlie Yates, to make a mess of it, and run up a score of seven in 1946.

The 15th is an altogether different kettle of fish, a 500-yarder with a decent-size fish kettle of a lake in front of the green. In 1956, Walker Inman caused considerable disturbance among the fish on his way to a 10.

The 16th is a good example of the law of physics which states that the distance a golf ball will fly is proportionate to the mass of the club-head times the square of its speed, except over water. In 1950, Herman Barron made the fundamental mistake of selecting a club suitable for an overland shot of 170 yards and he compounded his error by stubbornly insisting that the flight of golf ball through the air could not be affected by the nature of the elements at ground level. That folly cost him 11 strokes.

The 17th, 400 yards, is a dull hole, producing nothing but a dreary sequence of birdies and the occasional eagle. However, in 1963, the Spaniard Angel Miguel managed a seven.

And so to the climax of our exhibition round by the great masters of golf. At 405 yards, the 18th normally plays a drive and six-iron, being steeply uphill, and most tournament professionals would say that the main difficulty is the putting. The green is notorious for both speed and slope. Densmore Shute probably had a rider to add to that judgment after his eight in 1959, giving us an inward 86 for our eclectic score of nightmares.

I don't know about you but I find it a source of considerable comfort that some of the greatest players in the history of golf can go round Augusta National in 160 strokes. What is more, they all agree that with fairways 80 yards wide it is a doddle to make par; the problems only start when you try to manoeuvre your ball into positions from which you can claim birdies.

As for the eclectic low score of the Masters, I am pretty confident in asserting that every hole has yielded an eagle at some time so, with Gene Sarazen's albatross at the 15th in 1935, that would give a round of 35. Some people may consider this figure is a more suitable advertisement for the golf which has been played at the Masters. It is a matter of opinion. My feeling is that a score of 35 for 18 holes has less to do with golf than with freakish luck.

The Observer, 1984

In the Basque country

There is one small corner of Europe where golf runs strongly in the bloodstream, where the butcher and the baker and the candlestick-maker all know the difference between a mashie and a niblick and play the game as zealously as any Scottish community. When the Duke of Wellington's conquering army completed its Peninsula campaign it rested in the foothills of the Pyrenees in southern France, and some Scottish officers sought diversion by making a golf course at Pau. This is, of course, Basque country and the Basques are natural sportsmen. They seem to excel at all games. Nobody has the slightest idea where the Basques came from. Were they originally a gipsy tribe from eastern Europe? If so, why is their language similar to the tongue spoken by the Cornish? (Maybe the Cornish were part of the same tribe and simply moved on a bit further, across the Channel.) At all events the Basques have a natural eye for a ball and a gift for athletic prowess.

So golf flourished at Pau (from 1856) and pretty soon the Basques had another course at Biarritz, the fashionable resort for visiting English gentlefolk. Although golf was an amenity for the tourist it was also, simultaneously, a popular sport for the locals and this local enthusiasm resulted in the building of three more courses, La Nivelle, Chiberta and Chantaco at St Jean de Luz. This small area thus became the cradle of French golf, producing every native player of distinction including the only continental ever to have won the Open championship, Arnaud Massy.

As to the quality of the courses, nobody would put them in the highest championship class although all of them in their different ways are exceedingly pleasant. To play Pau is to step back into the 19th century. As you enter the old farmhouse club your pace slackens. You simply have to dawdle and inspect the photographs and paintings of the founding fathers, the picture of the coach and six which took the members off to play matches at Biarritz, the brown-varnished honour boards with the names of long dead captains in gold leaf.

The course is built on a flat pasture with the Pyrenees towering above. The mountains shelter the golf and on a hot sunny day, with the inevitable poplars shimmering in the heat, only a churl would criticise Pau for being on the short side. Perhaps to extract the full flavour of Pau it ought to be played with long-headed woods and gutta balls, with dinner in the club afterwards, of roast boar newly shot by a young officer of the line, and gallons of claret. Who will join me for this reconstruction?

Biarritz is my least favourite of the Basque courses. It has been the victim of urban development and is consequently rather crammed into its clifftop site and you can almost feel the marauding eyes of predatory property developers boring into your back as you play. It is very short, although it enjoys a considerable reputation among French golf enthusiasts.

I prefer Chiberta which has about it that important aura of quiet and detachment. It is well wooded and since it springs from the era when golf course architecture was becoming established as an art form, combined with sound principles of landscaping and golfing strategy, it has a quality to challenge the golfer's shot-making as well as the charm of the older courses.

Both these dimensions of quality and charm are to be found in differing degrees at La Nivelle and Chantaco. La Nivelle is built on wooded heathland and is potentially a fine course indeed. Golf courses are like wine in that the product must be laid down to mature. It will be some time before the connoisseur can make a judgment but I fancy that La Nivelle will develop into a course possessing all the elements which we look for in golf: beautiful surroundings, good underfoot conditions and high golfing qualities. It might even become a great course.

Chantaco, I believe, will never achieve greatness in that exacting sense although for me it surpasses even Pau for the capacity it has to provide pleasure for the visitor. The fairways meander over the gently rolling foothill country and every change in direction reveals another vista through the frame of noble trees. Finally the course flattens out and on a hot day your calf muscles are grateful for this civilised arrangement. It is a golf course – and this, surely, is the ultimate test of holiday golf – where you lose track of which hole you are playing and what's more, what score you are achieving. You don't care. You just want to enjoy the same experience tomorrow.

Homes Abroad, 1980

Genius of the duneland

Admittedly Jones is a common name but it is a considerable coincidence that this Welsh tribe should have given golf the game's greatest practitioner and finest writer (Robert Tyre Jones), the supreme teacher (Ernest Jones) and the most innovative architect (Robert Trent Jones).

The genius of the three unrelated Joneses set the standards for the modern game and their accomplishments will shape golf for generations to come.

Trent Jones is now putting his final brush strokes to his magnum opus, the course by which he is ultimately content to be judged as an architect. However, before discussing the New Ballybunion, it may be helpful to say something about the man himself, because to know the designer is to understand his work.

Jones was born of Welsh parents and the family emigrated from England when Trent was six, settling in Rochester, New York, in

1912. He became a scratch golfer in his teens but the combination of the frustrations of golf and his fierce competitive nature gave him stomach ulcers and persuaded him that he should not make a career as a professional golfer.

Fortuitously he met Donald Ross, the Scottish architect who was building Oak Hill, Rochester, and Trent was fascinated by watching how the Michelangelo of the profession combined subtlety and imagination with high technical skill. Ross encouraged the young Jones to consider course design as a worthy alternative to seeking fame as a player.

Jones's response was typically thorough and unconventional. He talked Cornell University into allowing him to take a hotch-potch course of academic studies of his own devising, with elements of civil engineering, architecture, agriculture, chemistry and liberal arts. He simultaneously enrolled in the Rochester School of Art and today his sketchpad is never far from his hand, a skill of immense value in his business because instead of explaining his vision in words he can show clients how he proposes to transform the landscape.

One of the earliest lessons which Jones learned about course design was that controversy was good for business. He quickly gained the reputation as a builder of monsters, long and tight courses, with huge, undulating greens so closely guarded by bunkers that the pin positions were virtually inaccessible. In fact the true hallmark of a Trent Jones course is its flexibility, with scope for moving the tee markers and pin positions so that any hole can be set up to play quite easily or with an abnormal degree of difficulty.

Naturally, the United States Golf Association, which shows a marked preference for courses which have been designed or re-modelled by Trent Jones, tends to use tough combinations, hence the epithet coined by disgruntled US Open competitors for 'the architect who hates golfers'. Jones takes it all philosophically. 'In fact I love golfers; that is why I build them good courses to play.'

When he remodelled Baltusrol in New Jersey for the 1954 US Open there was an outcry from the members and the committee finally bowed to the criticism and sent for Jones. They met on the tee of the fourth hole, a par-three played across a lake, and said that the hole was just too difficult. Jones borrowed a five-iron, hit the ball straight into the hole, handed the club back and said, 'I don't think so.' Since then Baltusrol has been used for two more Opens.

Jones was soon the busiest architect in the world, flying 300,000 miles a year to build his distinctive courses on every continent. Four architects turned down commissions to create a golf course for the Aga Khan in Sardinia on the grounds that it was physically impossible to build a golf course on the precipitous, rocky hills of

Pevero. Jones took on the job, dynamiting the tops off the mini-mountains and crushing the rock to create fairways in the valleys.

And so to county Limerick. Jones had never had an opportunity to work with links country and, when he saw the massive dunes of Ballybunion, he drooled.

The original Ballybunion is impressive enough, with fairways winding through mountainous dunes along the clifftop. The neighbouring land is even more spectacular, the dunes even higher and plunging steeply into mighty ravines. It is a peculiar geological formation, 170 acres of wild duneland spreading to the estuary of the river Cashel on a coastline which is otherwise formed of rocky cliffs.

As you walk the fairways, mostly through valleys, you are met by constantly changing views, over the pastoral Limerick countryside, across the estuary to distant Kerry, over the bay to the town of Ballybunion (a place best observed from a decent distance, I might add) or out over the Atlantic.

Not that golfers will spend too much time admiring the view because you need to concentrate your mind on the golf on this course. Trent Jones sought to make every hole indelibly memorable and that he has done. It blows pretty hard on this coast at times and I guarantee that within five years the New Ballybunion will be spoken of with awe by golfing pilgrims from all over the world.

Some will call it the greatest links in the world. Some will insist that it is unplayable. Some will assert that it is the most beautiful place on earth. Some will curse Trent Jones for building a hole of 612 yards into the prevailing hurricanes. Some, but not many, will hit that green in two shots and reckon this feat as their finest achievement in golf. Some will revere it as the ultimate test of shotmaking. Some will never complete the course, having run out of golf balls or patience.

The 12th hole, the product of Trent Jones's impish penchant for controversy, will become as famous as the 16th at Cypress. And for much the same reasons. You trudge and trudge up a winding path wondering what on earth possessed the architect to subject you to such an ordeal. Then, on arrival at the crest of the dune, you understand.

At least you do after a bit because at first sight all you see is the tee and a moonscape of dunes with nowhere to play, no fairway, no green. Then, 253 yards across a vast chasm, your eye catches a fluttering flag on the skyline. That is it. It is the most intimidating shot I have ever seen.

In favourable conditions it is theoretically possible to hit straight for the flag but you need the nerve of a Blondin to try it. So you chicken out and bite off less and less of that formidable carry.

149

You could in fact play it with two seven-irons, and it is a par-four, but could you face yourself in the shaving mirror afterwards? This above all is the hole which red-blooded golfers will travel across the world to pit themselves against and you should know that I hit a pearler and sank my putt for an eagle two on this hole. Admittedly I had to play it in my mind's eye since I had wisely left the clubs in the locker room when I walked the course with Trent Jones.

The Observer, 1984

On a fast boat to China

For one whose notions about China were limited to gravy-stained images of willow pattern plates the reality held few surprises. Add bags of clubs to those willow pattern figures and you would have a remarkably accurate picture of Chung Shan.

You traverse zig-zag bridges, willow trees flutter in the breeze, birds which could well be impressionistic doves fly around, and the half-way house where you buy your Coke is a pagoda. If you overlook the imported sanitary fittings in the clubhouse you could imagine yourself back in the Ming Dynasty.

It is, of course, a romanticised and westernised recreation of the tourist's vision of China and the real Chinese find it very peculiar. There used to be about half a dozen courses in China before the war, used almost exclusively by rich foreigners, and these symbols of western decadence were swept away after the communist revolution.

Deng Xiaoping's reformist policies of opening up the country to tourism included the provision of 14 golf clubs and Henry Fok, a Hong Kong businessman, was quick off the mark. He obtained the rights to reintroduce golf to China after its 40-year banishment and he sent for Arnold Palmer.

Chung Shan, literally Middle Mountain, has been a place of pilgrimage for centuries, first for the curative properties of its hot springs and later for the faithful comrades to visit the birthplace of the father of the Republic, Sun Yat-sen. Now the pilgrimage to the Chung Shan hot springs resort will be mainly golfers, predominantly

Japanese since they are equally hooked on golf and communal bathing, although I suspect that the Scandinavians will quickly follow once the word gets round.

The building of the course presented some novel problems for the representatives of Arnold Palmer's design company. All the work had to be done by hand and 1000 people at 50 pence a day were recruited for the purpose. First there was a philosophical dilemma to be resolved. In this area of Guangdong province every available square foot of land is cultivated. The purpose of the earth is to grow food. You till the earth, trample in the right soil and plant rice or vegetables. From the golf course all you can see right to the horizon is a vast patchwork of tiny plots.

This is the way it has always been although the 20th century is represented by the occasional polythene tunnel cloche. Since you cannot eat grass, or flowers, or trees, the instinct of the work force was to grub them out. It was flying in the face of nature to cultivate them.

Having no concept of what a golf course might be, or for what purpose, or how it should look, the workers applied pastoral common sense to their task. Since the imperialist lunatics said that they were going to mow the grass around these curious pits of sand, it would make the job easier if we built them with straight sides. Squares and rectangles would be a vast improvement on those silly oval shapes.

Then came the débâcle of the irrigation system. Basically it was the same thing as piping water to a paddy field so they installed it above ground, with the pipes spreading like spaghetti over the fairways and the pop-up sprinklers rising into the air in the manner of sunflowers.

The spirits of ancestors also impeded the work for there were tombs on the site and the outrage of descendants had to be mollified by negotiation and compensation.

The work was finally done, and well done, as can be seen from the finest greens and tees to be found in the East, always a sure sign that the most important parts of a golf course, the unseen elements below the surface, have received proper attention.

At 6,600 yards it is an interesting and very demanding course off the back tees. The first par-five has come in for some criticism because water hazards demand that it be played with a driver and two seven-irons, although I do not subscribe to the convention that the golfer has an inalienable right to hit a fairway wood for his second shot on a long hole. I prefer the unfashionable view that the golfer should first have to solve the riddle of how best to play the hole before reaching for a club.

Peter Tang from Royal Hong Kong Golf Club is the visiting pro and national coach to the newly formed China Golf Association. He has selected 10 boys and 10 girls on the basis of their sporting aptitude at school. They live in dormitories at the club, have their own school and receive intense daily coaching in return for performing odd jobs on the course.

The nearby Shenzen course, designed by Isao Aoki for a Japanese consortium, operates a different training system. About 90 youngsters have been sent to Japan to train as caddies. By the end of this year, six courses will be ready for play and by 1990, when China hosts the Asian Games, it is hoped that native-born players will be good enough to take the gold medal for golf. That strikes me as a rashly optimistic target although Tang's pupils are making good progress. One of the girls in particular looks to be an excellent prospect.

Getting to Chung Shan sounds daunting although in practice it is not difficult. Visas can be obtained through travel agents and the next step is a 50-minute hydrofoil trip from Hong Kong across the South China Sea to the Portuguese enclave of Macao, where gambling is legal along with other vices, including formula three motor racing.

The bureaucracy and red tape is tedious, almost as bad as for British subjects entering Australia, but there is no culture shock involved in crossing the Chinese border. This is a designated economic zone and looks like any other scruffy oriental suburb with supermarkets, beggars and ads for Marlboro cigarettes. However, you then go through a control post into the real China of paddy fields and oxen and ramshackle bamboo huts for a 45-minute drive to the club.

The golf is good value by Hong Kong standards, about £17 a day. Some Hong Kong residents have taken out membership because it is cheaper than joining a club such as the Royal, even taking into account the hydrofoil journey and the overnight hotel room. The routine is to go over on Friday evening, rave it up in Macao and play golf on Saturday and Sunday.

According to legend Henry Fok built Chung Shan in a fit of pique when his membership of Royal Hong Kong was suspended because he tipped a waiter. The truth is more prosaic. He happens to own the hydrofoil company and one of the Macao casinos and his investment looks like turning into another profitable operation. It might incidentally be the seed from which China flowers as a major golfing nation.

The Observer, 1986

For those in peril on the deep

Admittedly, birds have got it all over golfers when it comes to comparing their abilities to fly. Also it must be conceded, that in the matter of getting home, birds have a sense of direction which is infinitely superior to that of the average golfer, especially after the club annual dinner.

In every other respect golfers are better than birds and come well above them in any sensible order of precedence among living creatures. Being magnanimous – and whoever heard of a magnanimous magpie? – we golfers are reasonably tolerant of birds, steering a middle course between the extremes of blasting them to smithereens with shotguns and eating vegetarian pie for Christmas dinner.

Likewise, the golfer is generally content to adopt a live and let live policy towards the rabbit, a creature of few if any redeeming qualities unless it is snugly secure beneath a crisp pie crust.

Yet birds and rabbits have joined forces to wage war against the harmless golfer and, sad to relate, they have scored some crushing victories against an endangered species of oddball golfer.

Lighthouse keepers live a fairly oddball life by normal standards. It is probably not true to say that all they have to do is throw a switch at six o'clock in the evening, although for the life of me I cannot think of any other urgent duty except switching it off again in the morning. Be that as it may, they do have spare moments between their important contribution to marine safety and, in cases where they are fortunate enough to serve lighthouses standing on foundations covered by turf, they like to create golf courses. Naturally. After all, fishing is about the only other form of recreation available and since the average fisherman spends 99.9 per cent of his time not catching fish the hobby has a low rating as physical exercise.

The light on the Isle of May in the North Sea controls the entrance to the Firth of Forth and the keepers built themselves a sporty three-holer which they could truthfully describe as being something between the Old Course at St Andrews and the championship links of Muirfield.

The birds and the rabbits put a stop to all that. Puffins and rabbits are concerned with only three activities, eating, digging and procreation and, being blissfully free of predators, they went at it with abandon until the turf was so honeycombed with burrows that the soil cover was destroyed. Today there are no families living on the Isle of May and the golf course has disappeared.

Rabbits also played hell with the nine-hole course made by the lighthouse keepers on the Calf of Man. The trouble, they told me, was that you got a hole-in-one with almost every shot. Heather encroached onto the course and today the station's only two oddball golfers, Andrew Marshal and Denis Hemsley, are restricted to hitting practice shots in a field, all very different from the great days when the keepers played for the open championship of the Irish Sea every Sunday morning.

But golf still thrives on the rocky outposts of the British Isles. Fairisle has two lighthouses, north and south, and although the island is only three miles long and half a mile wide it has some 60 inhabitants who pause in their knitting from time to time to play golf. They also, presumably, eat rabbits so the nine-hole course has a chance.

Naturally, the main competition of the year is the inter-lighthouse championship which carries a handsome trophy. They are honest folk, these North Sea dwellers and not given to flights of pretension. When I asked about the quality of the course I received the answer in one word: rough.

The major hazard with lighthouse golf, apart from the depredations of rabbits, are outcrops of rock. These can prove very expensive in golf balls if the bounce goes the wrong way and this factor adds greatly to the interest of the latest addition to the golfing facilities of the Northern Lighthouse Board.

It is a four-hole course on the island of Hyskeir out in the northern Atlantic approaches, an outpost measuring half a mile by 500 yards when the tide is low. The tee shots tend to get a bit tight and tense at high water but Hyskeir is reckoned to be a good test at any time and considerable ingenuity, not to mention dedicated work, has gone into its construction.

It has, for instance, five tees so the eighth hole is quite different from the fourth when you come to play it the second time around. The tees are not just flattish areas of grass like, say, at the Old Course but properly built up platforms in the best Robert Trent Jones manner.

The first hole measures 60-yards, often calling for a good chip into the prevailing hurricane, and finesse is paramount on the 30-yard second. Then you come to the Long Hop Out, all of 120 yards, followed by the tricky 100-yard fourth. From the alternative tee across a footbridge it measures 140-yards.

The course was started three years ago and the building involved returfing in parts to cover the more inconvenient rocky outcrops. It is said to be settling down quite nicely. In theory there is scope for extension but the keepers have no plans for new holes because it would mean disturbing the wildfowl.

That is a positively saintly attitude in my view, considering the way that bird life has devastated other lighthouse courses. There is only one major problem about running a balanced golfing pro-gramme at Hyskeir: four of the keepers are avid golfers but, rotas being what they are, there are never more than three of them on that island at the same time. Therefore they can never experience the unique joy of foursomes golf.

Hang on. Perhaps they can. What if they all hit two balls off the tee. Then B and C can each have a second shot at one of A's balls, and so on. Yes, it would work and the winning partnership could qualify for two first prizes in the event of a tie, since it would be impractical for the AB team to play off against the BA team. Just imagine the gambling potential of such a game. The imagination boggles. It might be a bit slow playing six balls, but that would not matter on Hyskeir since they would not be holding up anybody behind. We might be on to a winner with this one. I hereby give the world a new form of golf and christen it Lighthouse.

The Observer, 1987

One millennium should do it

It is, I venture to suggest, quite impossible to play golf under water and yet I would like to preface my remarks with a very short lesson in marine biology, for one aspect of this subject is of concern to golfers. I refer to coral, a living organism which flourishes in warm seas.

Now I do not wish to engage in a theosophical debate about the nature of the universe, or to offend religious susceptibilities about the meaning and purpose of life, so I will confine myself to discussion of nature.

In this context I see nature as an extremely foresighted planner who understood very well that in time man would despoil the environment with tower blocks, concrete jungles, stinking motor cars, stock exchanges and nuclear stockpiles. In order to maintain his sanity and his health man would preserve small oases of natural landscape and play golf on them. Occasionally, man would come so close to losing his marbles entirely under the stress of modern living that he would have to get right away from everything, to relax playing golf, drinking rum punches, listening to distant steel bands and swimming in warm oceans. Therefore, Nature invented coral, which quietly worked away in the shale seas of the Caribbean, growing a millimetre a day against the time when man would need this sanctuary.

So grew the string of islands off the eastern seaboard of the Americas. The islands grew and became covered in dense vegetation and men populated them, mostly escaped slaves, and these men developed into a race of beautiful and gentle and intelligent people who grew sugar and played cricket very well. Quite recently, a second ago in the timescale of evolution, the purpose of the Caribbean islands was finally realised; they became the paradise of golfers. Nature's plan was revealed in all its glory and we could finally appreciate the grand design of nature, for coral was invented specifically to make golf courses.

Coral is relatively soft until it becomes exposed to the air, no matter what you might think if you graze your leg on a coral reef while scuba diving. It is therefore a simple task to drive a heavy bulldozer through jungles growing on coral rock and, hey presto, fairway. Crush the coral and you have subsoil for your grass. Crush it finer and you have a bunker sand so white that it glares in the tropical sun. Oh wondrous crustacean, you are destined to delight the tired golfer, for coral courses are the most beautiful of all golf's treasury of land and seascapes.

In some, but not all, coral courses the bulldozer in its progress through the lush vegetation has pushed huge boulders of coral into what we would normally call the rough. In these instances there is no rough, for the fairway runs right up against tropical jungle, with this fringe of boulders overgrown by ferns and bushes and trees and absolutely impenetrable. Local rules permit the golfer whose ball has strayed off the ribbon of prepared turf to drop another ball, without penalty, opposite the point where his original ball had disappeared into this wall of jungle. I was once playing with a quick-tempered solicitor in Freeport, at the lovely King's Inn course, when he impulsively threw his club in disgust after hitting a bad shot. The club rattled into the undergrowth. His caddie dutifully ventured into the dark vegetation but could not find the club. 'Hang on,' said my companion. 'Stay in there and I will throw another club in exactly the same way. See where this second one lands and then you will find the first one.' The net result was that both clubs were never seen again. The surprise was that the caddie managed to find his way out.

As to whereabouts in the Caribbean you should go for your

initiation into this exotic and superb form of golf, I do not think it matters very much.

The sun can be trusted to shine benignly on all the islands and the sea to be equally receptive to an overheated golfing body. Planter's Punch is universal and for those golfers who like to fish – and it is quite extraordinary how often these two disparate hobbies appeal to the same man – there is nothing in my experience to compare with hooking into a big ray or kingfish in these Caribbean waters.

We are seeking to restore the tissues ravaged by modern living and, while the Caribbean islands cover a wide variety of political, social and national affiliations, there is a mood and easy pace of life which embraces the entire area. The Caribbean style is Mid Atlantic, a mix of British, American and local influences, and this cosmopolitan atmosphere is reflected in the hotels where honest ale and roast beef are generally as equally available as abalone steaks and Manhattans. On a practical note, whichever island takes your fancy I would look around for a package trip in order to take full advantage of the reduced travel and accommodation charges.

Bermuda is not strictly Caribbean at all but I must include it in this general survey if only to commend the glorious Mid Ocean golf club, an exhilarating course along the clifftops with fabulous views (and shots) over the ocean. Tobago is a tiny island and for the visiting golfer there is just the hotel, the course and the ocean, which is perfect if you are looking for the quiet holiday, although not to the taste of those who like to go out raving it up in different clubs each night.

Jamaica and Barbados have a slightly British emphasis in their golf, inherited from their colonial past, while the Bahamas on the whole have a distinctly American flavour about the golf. I have a special feeling for Great Harbour Cay, just a hop from Miami and indeed within easy range of a day visit, because I went there when the first coral boulder was pushed aside by the bulldozers and then returned to find this beautiful little island made even more beautiful by ribbons of green fairways and a tasteful bungalow hotel. Take your pick but do take my advice and try Caribbean golf once before you shuffle off this globe. It is an experience you will never forget or regret.

Homes Abroad, 1981

When history is bunkers

According to the latest statistics, the longest driver on the American tour is Fred Couples, who has recently supplanted Dan Pohl from the top of the table. Couples' average this year is 277.1 yards and that of course includes a significant proportion of bounce and roll. He probably averages a carry nearer 255 yards. That is a healthy whack but it would not be long enough to fly the fairway bunker at the remodelled eighth hole of the Augusta National course.

By extending the tee 20 yards the club has fundamentally changed the character of this 535-yard par-five. Among the elite company of golfers who are good enough to win invitations to play in the Masters, and that means the best in the world, there are only a handful powerful enough to attempt that carry of 260 yards.

By really winding themselves up and cranking out their Sunday special blue-flamers I suppose that Raymond Floyd, Sandy Lyle, Andy Bean, Lon Hinkle, Greg Norman and Severiano Ballesteros could have reasonable expectations of making the carry in still air. Fuzzy Zoeller is having trouble with his back at the moment but when he is in good physical nick he could be added to the list.

This means that all the others are put at a huge disadvantage. With no chance of making the carry they must, in certain conditions, take three-woods off the tee in order to ensure that they do not run into the bunker. That in turn puts any thought of reaching the green with a second shot out of the question.

Of course, it can be argued that this is only right and proper. The hole is a par-five and should be played with three strokes from tee to green. However we know how the original designers, Bobby Jones and Dr Alastair Mackenzie, intended the hole to be played. Their idea was to present the golfer with two challenges. First, he must decide on the tee whether to summon up the nerve and the muscle to attempt the carry, or risk driving into the narrow funnel of fairway alongside the bunker, or to play short. Now, if he should select the first option, and if he should succeed, he is rewarded by another ticket in the lottery. He can choose between having a rip at the green or playing safely short. There are severe penalties for failure, specially if the error is to the left as it is likely to be because a hooking shot is the usual penalty for pressing.

This delicate balance between reward and punishment was what made the hole so exciting for spectators and so daunting for the players. That balance, in my view, has now been destroyed except for those six exceptional golfers. For the vast majority the hole is now an unexceptional three-shotter and the only requirement of the second shot is to move the ball forward. Birdie opportunities are limited to the possibility of pitching close enough for a single putt.

When Gene Sarazen first played the Augusta National course he told Bobby Jones that all the par-fives could be played with a putter off the tee. It was a typically contentious Sarazen thrust, with just enough truth in it to provoke a lively discussion. In the case of the eighth hole today Sarazen's criticism is almost valid. Of Augusta's four long holes, the second and eighth could well be played by clipping a putter off the tee about 100 yards. The 13th and 15th are beautifully balanced holes where all but the short hitters can have a go at the greens with high risk second shots.

The first hole, a par-four, has also had 10 yards added to the driving length, now requiring a carry of 250 yards over the fairway bunker. In this case there is still a reasonable target of fairway alongside the bunker but it offers a much more difficult approach angle to the green. That is as it should be, for the reward to the brave who fly the sand is a much improved chance to hit the approach shot close to the flag.

At this golf course the changes will be closely analysed and if the findings endorse my instinctive feelings about them we may be sure that restoration measures will be taken. The lengthening of these two holes inevitably led to much comment by the players, most of it along the lines that there is too much monkeying around with classic golf courses these days, and that masterpieces of design by the great architects of the past should be preserved in their original form.

The intention behind such protest is admirable, but that intention is not served by setting golf courses in the amber of conservation. Donald Ross is frequently cited as an architect whose work should not be touched by so much as the planting of a single bush which did not appear on his plans. Ross worked in the days of hickory shafts and so his courses were built to a scale which the game of golf has outgrown. By preserving his courses exactly the way he built them we are actually destroying them because his genius lay in creating shot values. That is the architect's job. A Donald Ross short hole which he designed to be played with a three-iron is a completely different hole now that golfers using improved equipment play it with a six-iron. What we have to conserve is his long iron shot and that can only be done by changing the hole. Golf courses are living, growing entities and must be continually adjusted in order to keep them the way they were, just as a hedge has to be clipped regularly to keep it the same.

It is not just a case of pushing the tees further and further back;

that preserves only the shot value of the drive. Improvements are just as necessary for approach play, which means that adjustments must be made to bunkers and other hazards in order to preserve the integrity of the architect's concept.

Nowhere is this better understood, and better implemented, than at Augusta and hundreds of changes have been made to the course in the past 50 years in order to keep it the way Jones planned. I very much hope that when I return next April I shall be able to watch all the competitors anxiously following the progress of their drives at the eighth, wincing as the ball kicks up a shell burst of sand as it smacks into the fairway bunker, or exhaling with relief as it pitches on the fairway beyond the hazard and bounces towards the green.

The Observer, 1981

Chapter 7
In the present tense

Christy O'Connor

At a recent golf tournament in Ireland a visitor took up his position behind two priests. As a matter of incidental intelligence you always take up position behind priests at Irish tournaments. They have a highly developed technique (compounded by exploiting the natural deference due to their cloth with some brisk work with their elbows) of insinuating themselves to the forefront of galleries.

Anyway, this visitor was startled to hear one priest ask of his companion, 'Who's that playing with Himself?' The visitor looked down the fairway in shocked surprise. With his ear not yet attuned to the native idiom, he had not immediately understood that the question was merely an inquiry as to the name of Christy O'Connor's playing partner.

In Ireland, in a golfing context, it is unnecessary to use the name of O'Connor. It is Himself. That is enough to denote the most famous sporting hero the Irish nation has produced and one of the few overseas players to make an impact on the American sporting public without actually joining the US tour. This has been done mainly with a long string of Ryder Cup appearances.

At home, Himself is held in public esteem as a secular saint. The volume of gallery support is generally reckoned to be worth two shots a round to O'Connor. And the weight of prayers for his short putts, in the opinion of opponents, puts him at risk of a penalty for outside assistance.

People see O'Connor differently. To some he is a quiet, shy man. To some, a hell-raising extrovert, eager for a fist-fight. To some, a moody bore. To some, a warm and witty companion.

Everyone agrees that he is a superb golfer, but as to the man himself there are as many O'Connors as there are people who think they know him. O'Connor does nothing to clarify this situation. He is a very private person and takes the rather old-fashioned view that while he may be a public figure on the golf course, everything else about him is entirely his own business.

In a literal sense there are two Christy O'Connors on the golf circuit, which makes life tiresome in reporting tournaments. There is Himself and his nephew, with the same name, the same darkly handsome appearance and – dare I predict? – the same potential for golfing success. But we are concerned with Christy senior – and that is quite enough O'Connors to try to unscramble.

The most important thing about O'Connor is that he is Irish, and that condition implies more, much more, than a straight label of citizenship. To be Irish is to ingest the tormented history of that race with your mother's milk. You are weaned on the Orange repression and thus rebellion (against authority in all its forms) is instilled in the cradle; Cromwell's repression cauterizes those areas of the brain which deal in logic, the Easter Rebellion puts fire into your heart, and the potato famine puts a chip on your shoulder.

Other factors work their mischief in the making of an Irishman. County Galway, which is O'Connor country, is a dark and mysterious area of inhospitable mountains where to till the land the coastal folk first have to create the very soil by mixing sand from the beach with seaweed and waiting for the rains to wash away the salty sourness. Poverty is, then, another chromosome in the genetic chain of the Irish. The simple struggle to survive has left its mark. So has religion. And so, above all, has the native Gaelic imprint of mysticism and feckless joy. Irishness is both a blessing and a curse.

The Irish, who dearly love a myth, are content to accept that Christy sprang onto the scene as a young professional, full-grown and with a God-given swing, and immediately began to win fortune for himself and fame for his race.

The prosaic truth is that Christy learned the rudiments of golf while caddying in Galway and subsequently moved, via Killarney, to Royal Dublin Golf Club. O'Connor's swing was far from natural. People who watch his smooth rhythm, with the minimum of fuss in assessing the shot, are led to believe that his swing is an inborn talent, requiring neither thought nor practice. The notion is absurd, although these days O'Connor's pre-match routine consists of hitting no more than half a dozen shots to capture the 'feel' of his swing.

As a young man it was his habit to take himself off to Dublin Bay and hit golf balls off the sand for hour after hour. If you have ever tried to hit a golf ball off sea-washed sand you will know that there is only one way to do it: by clipping the ball cleanly off the surface. Try hitting down and through, in the way you take a divot off grass, and you break a wrist. Here was the genesis of the O'Connor swing and the technique which earned him the nickname of Wristy Christy. Here too, no doubt, was implanted the seed of unpredictability which has made O'Connor such an in-and-out player all his life. When his immaculate timing is slightly off, O'Connor's game suffers more than most. The so-called modern method, with a long extension down and through the ball, gives a golfer some margin of error when his timing is astray. But when O'Connor is firing sweetly, flicking the ball away with a combination of power and artistry, he is a match for anyone.

O'Connor's early reputation was based on his inordinate length. As a young man he gloried in the strength of his athletic frame and there is hardly a club in Ireland where they do not recall an example of tremendous hitting.

With maturity came wisdom. 'Nowadays I drive for position and I don't mind that I have to sacrifice a bit of length.' Today, as he approaches 50, O'Connor's shoulders are rounded in a 'golfer's stoop', permanently hunched into the address position. He occasionally suffers from arthritic pains in the joints. Even so, on his day he still plays better than most. Pros look for his name on the leader board with apprehension, knowing that he can win any tournament.

He is feared less for his stroke-making than for the intangible – but far more important – qualities of his character. His record is impressive enough, with several important victories every year of his competitive career. He won the first four-figure cheque in the history of British golf and, much later, won the first five-figure cheque. But dig a little deeper into the statistics and the essential hardness of O'Connor emerges. Nearly all his triumphs have been achieved with a low last round when the pressure is making the others falter.

If the wind blows – they call it O'Connor weather – the pros recognise that the dice are loaded in favour of Himself. Where others are fighting the elements and slogging at full-bore with a six-iron, O'Connor will take his three-iron and outwit the gale. The harder it blows the more quietly he seems to play his shots.

On a windy day in Ireland, before his home crowd, O'Connor is reckoned to be virtually unbeatable – given two other conditions. The first premise is that his putting must be in good order, and that is totaly unpredictable. Some days he holes everything with an inspired flair, other times he cannot putt worth a cuss.

The other pre-condition, possibly related to the first at times, concerns the sensitive subject of how he has spent the previous evening. There is an Irish tradition that drinking is not so much an aid to conviviality as an end in itself. The idea, not to put too fine a point on it, is to get plastered.

It matters little that O'Connor is reasonably temperate by nature. He enjoys a social drink as much as the next man, but no more than that. The point is that every Irishman wants to buy Christy a drink. It is a national ambition, a duty. And since there are even more Irishmen abroad than there are in Ireland he can never escape.

Americans may ask: If this O'Connor is such a hell of a golfer why isn't he up there with Palmer and Nicklaus? It is a valid question and deserves a rational answer, if one can be found. The answer lies partly in ambition. O'Connor prefers a modest life-style. He still lives in the same house he bought when he first moved to Dublin as a young man. By Irish standards he is wealthy enough. He has all the fame he can handle.

But there is another reason and it resides in a dilemma which every talented golfer must face and resolve. The Bitch Goddess of Success is a demanding mistress. For every bounty she bestows she demands a sacrifice.

You want to make a million? Very well, you may. But in the process you must cut yourself off from your friends and the warm associations of your social circle. You must subjugate your family to your career. You must wander the world and make speeches and live among the kings and mandarins of commerce. You must, in short, deny your birthright. To an Irishman, a *real* Irishman, the proposition is unthinkable.

Christy O'Connor, the private man, has settled for a more modest but happier way of golf – and life.

Golf World, 1982

Severiano Ballesteros

There was a large crowd around the first tee of the Augusta National Golf Club last year. The mood was one of curiosity and excited anticipation. The experienced golf watchers in the gallery appraised the young man standing on the tee. A good build for a golfer: perhaps a shade on the tall side at just over six feet but with a powerful physique and a long, broad back like Arnold Palmer.

That Palmer image would shortly be reinforced even more strongly. The women in the audience surely noticed more about this boy. A good-looking kid in an old-fashioned way, with his dark colouring and the face reflecting a certain darkness of the soul. A handsome, matinee idol face reminiscent of the young Ray Milland with brooding eyes which he kept focused on the middle distance most of the time.

His fellow competitor, Tom Weiskopf, possibly shared the general curiosity about this Severiano Ballesteros but, if so, he managed to conceal it. He stood aside as the Spaniard teed up. Weiskopf looked unimpressed, as he had every right so to do. After all, he had often played with youngsters who had burst onto the golfing scene with a big reputation. Most of them had enjoyed their brief notoriety and then faded into oblivion, while the Weiskopfs and the Nicklauses and the Players endured for year after year.

Ballesteros addressed the ball, holding his hands well out from his body, too far out for the purists. Another touch of unorthodoxy as the Spaniard executed his backswing with no thought of keeping his right elbow in. He let the elbow fly high as he coiled back in a wide arc. The swing itself gave no appearance of effort. The boy was no slugger. He swished the club through the ball as if cutting the head from a daisy. The audience reaction was a massed intake of breath in an audible gasp, followed by an 'AAAh!' and then cannonade of applause.

Weiskopf permitted one of his eyebrows to rise a millimetre, the outward manifestation of a reaction which he later explained had almost caused him to fall over in surprise.

'It was the sweetest three hundred-yard drive into a stiff headwind you ever saw,' he said later. When it was his turn to hit, Weiskopf was still unsettled by his first sight of Ballesteros in action, to the extent that he himself carved his drive into the trees.

So this was the Ballesteros who had taken America by storm the week previously by playing in his first PGA Tour event, the Greater Greenboro Open, and winning it in cavalier style to add to the sixteen international victories he had achieved in different parts of the world before his 21st birthday.

By now there are few places in the free, or golfing world where the name of Ballesteros is not familiar. Oddly, one country where he remains virtually unknown is his native Spain, where golf has not become a national obsession. And it was because of the lack of golf tradition in Spain that Ballesteros became the most exciting young player in the game.

Spanish professionals have achieved quite a reputation in recent years, as evidence the World Cup results, and nearly all of them have come up the same way. They started as boy caddies, serving the tourists and the few wealthy Spaniards who have taken to the game.

Spanish golf is enlightened in that a comprehensive training scheme operates for the boy caddies at most clubs, with a proper schoolroom and teacher on the premises so that general education continues daily, as well as professional instruction in golfing matters. In their spare time, while waiting around for clients, the boys chip balls around, in the traditional manner of boy caddies everywhere. They play on the course in the evenings when the work is over and after six or seven years of this regime they emerge as highly competent pros.

That, indeed, is very much how Manuel Ballesteros became a

tournament professional. His young brother Severiano was different, in that he never enrolled as an official caddie.

Naturally, with his brother a pro and living near the golf club at Santander in northern Spain, near Bilbao, Severiano – or Sevvy as he has become universally known – used to hang about the club and join in the games of the caddies, chipping for peseta sidebets or, often enough, for a cigarette as the prize. Nobody told him how to hold a club, or how it should be swung. He did not read instruction books for the simple reason that such things do not exist in Spain.

Manuel gave him an old three-iron but that was the extent of his fraternal assistance. He did not teach Sevvy because Sevvy did not want to be taught. He learned on the basis of 'monkey see, monkey do', watching the way the good golfers did it and copying them, insofar that this process conformed with his own instincts about how to swing a club. He was allowed to play in the annual caddies' contest and at the age of 15 he won it.

One of the members, a low handicap player with enough substance to indulge in a modest patronage, took an interest in Sevvy's progress and encouraged him to apply himself to the game. The club agreed that Sevvy could play on the course in the evenings, although by this time he had long since been sneaking out to remote parts of the course when things were quiet to play a few holes.

This solitary apprenticeship during his formative years confirmed Sevvy's philosophy of golf. Most youngsters are tutored by established golfers who, from the depth of their experience, pass on advice about how vital it is from time to time to play safe. Words like 'lay up' and 'lag' and 'the fat of the green' have come into the game's vocabulary as expressions of the essential caution which is the key to low, consistent scoring.

Sevvy never heard those words when he was playing by himself. He employed juvenile logic: golf is a game of taking as few strokes as possible; the shortest distance between two points is a straight line; therefore the best way to play golf is to play directly at the flag whenever possible. If trees or water intervene, then fly the ball over them.

Nothing that has happened in later years of tournament golf has caused Sevvy to revise that attitude in any marked degree. He says: 'With me it is eagle or a seven. Sometimes it comes to be a seven but I take the risk.' This refreshing approach, echoes of the young Palmer again, is what makes Sevvy so exciting to watch, as much as the sheer animal strength of his golf.

After winning the club caddie tournament for the second year, and by now able to beat par regularly over the Santander course, Sevvy's patron bank-rolled him for his first tilt at tournament golf. The 17-

year-old travelled over the border to attempt to prequalify for the Portuguese Open, ran up an horrendous score and returned home chastened but more determined than ever to make his mark on the game. He was soon back on the European circuit and acquiring a reputation and modest place money with his slam-bang golf.

The wider world of golf really began to take note of the Spanish prodigy when he played in the British Open at Royal Birkdale in 1976 and turned it into a two-man chase between himself and Johnny Miller. As everyone knows, Miller's superior golfing savvy narrowly prevailed over Sevvy's direct methods on that occasion but the youngster had definitely arrived.

Far from being disappointed at the outcome, after the initial trauma of being pipped at the post, the Open added the final ingredient to Sevvy's golfing armoury, confidence in his own abilities. The natural diffidence of a young man in a strange environment, able to speak nothing but his native Spanish, vanished overnight to be replaced by a jaunty assurance which grew week by week. The rest of the story is written in the record books. Victory in the Dutch Open championship shortly after that Birkdale Open started a triumphant trail around the world, in Europe, in Africa, in Japan and then in the United States.

Greensboro began a new chapter in the Ballesteros saga and a political struggle of such proportions that at times Sevvy regretted that he had ever won that tournament. The issue arose because the PGA Tour has rules requiring a golfer to obtain a card, granted after a playing test at the qualifying school, before he can compete without restriction in PGA events. Now that Ballesteros had won Greensboro and had qualified for the Tournament of Champions, every sponsor wanted the exciting youngster in his field.

The PGA quickly granted Ballesteros permission to play the Tournament of Champions and offered to give him a card without the formality of a playing test. However, there are strings attached to that precious pasteboard, notably that a golfer may seek only three exemptions to compete overseas, in conflict with US official events, in any one season, except in the case of his home circuit.

Ballesteros was eager to continue his successful career in Europe and elsewhere and so he advanced the claim that his home circuit was Europe. No, said the PGA, your home circuit is Spain (which has only two major events a year). Offer and counter-offer followed rejection and counter-rejection. Ballesteros became the pawn in a complex game of chess and another commotion broke around his head when the USGA gave him a special invitation to compete in the 1978 US Open championship at Cherry Hills. Some American professionals were miffed that the Spaniard should be so privileged while they had to play their way into the championship through the qualifying rounds.

In the event Sevvy amply justified his invitation by his play. Negotiations with the PGA continued, with Sevvy demanding the best of both worlds. He wanted to play his 15 American tournaments and he also wanted to be free to plunder Europe as before, a specially attractive idea since on the European circuit he is permitted to demand appearance money and guarantees which make his golf profitable every week, win or lose. The outcome? – he has declined the invitation to become a PGA Tour regular in 1979, but he will be making several US appearances throughout the season including the US Open.

During his brief career Sevvy has shown himself to be acutely aware of the value of a dollar, or a yen or a Deutschmark. When he was selected to represent the team of the continental Europeans against the British Isles for the Hennessy Cup match he first demanded an appearance fee and then, as the date of the match approached, he raised the ante before he would consent to play. In the same vein, he announced that he would not be available to represent Spain for the third time in the World Cup, although he had been in the winning team the previous two years and had been decorated by the King of Spain for his services to sport, because the cash rewards were derisory for a professional.

These days it is fashionable to excuse such characteristics in a golfer, putting the blame for venality onto their managers. In Sevvy's case he makes no bones about his belief that the labourer is worthy of his hire and that he is a very expensive grade of labourer. This hunger, which converts into grinding determination on the golf course, also causes him at times to act the prima donna, snapping sharply at indiscreet photographers who snap at him at inopportune moments, and he tends to dramatic posturing. Sometimes he glowers when he misses a putt, or gazes reproachfully up to the sky when a shot goes astray, as if to put the blame where it lies, but many a good man before him has indulged in youthful histrionics.

Sevvy is getting better and for the most part, when he is going well, his naturally sunny disposition makes him the delight of the galleries and his playing companions. Off the course he is friendly and agreeable, given to jokes and verbal by-play which is so much a part of the locker room life. As his English improves – and he is now at the stage where he is beginning to use idiom with a certain fluency and precision – so his personality is more faithfully revealed. And he is a great favourite with the girls. Part of the Ballesteros phenomenon in Europe has been the invasion of golf tournaments by teenage girls who clearly have not the slightest interest in golf but do have an overwhelming interest in Sevvy. Groupies in golf. What would Harry Vardon have said about that?

For a young man with a talent of this magnitude, the actual playing is possibly the least of his worries. He can handle a tricky par-four but can he handle the success which comes his way? Sevvy is learning fast and acquiring a graciousness which was missing in his teenage days. He is also becoming adept at handling his press conferences, parrying the awkward question with a bland response which would do credit to a politician.

As for the future, we can only guess at what he will do and how he will fare. He could burn himself out with his punishing schedule, for he has a problem with his back caused and aggravated by excessive golf. If he does opt to play in America as a regular member of the Tour in 1980 he just might find that homesickness has such a detrimental effect on his play that he could not win. He is a gregarious young man, never happier than when he is in the convivial company of his fellow Spanish professionals, and that will surely weigh heavily in his decisions. He enjoys playing occasional tournaments in America but does not want to settle down, like Bruce Devlin or David Graham. And by historical precedent, always accepting Gary Player as the exception which proves the rule, foreign golfers do not prosper in America unless they cut their home ties and become residents.

However, the one certainty about Ballesteros which those who know him have come to accept, is that nothing is certain about him. He is a law unto himself. He breaks all the rules of what is or what is not possible. There is no predicting with him. All you can say is that here is an extremely tough young man with an outsize talent for golf and, as such, it is entirely on the cards that he could shortly be the dominating player in America just as he has subdued the worlds of golf in Europe and the Far East.

US Open Programme, 1979

Howard Clark

Cocktail parties and receptions have become as much a part of golf tournaments as the practice round and, shameful admission, I am not very good at them, being short on social graces and polite small talk. It always happens sooner or later that some kindly intentioned person takes pity on the morose oaf hovering on the fringe of the gathering and advances brightly with the standard opening gambit: 'Who do you want to win?'

That is when I spill sherry down my tie. I would find it very difficult to nominate a player I would prefer not to win; it could hardly be different after having spent most of my life being around them week after week since they first played in the Boys' championship.

For all that I must confess to a special pleasure at the run of success by Howard Clark this year, with his wins in the Madrid and Spanish Opens and runner-up in the match-play championship, elevating him to 24th in the world rankings.

If ever a golfer deserved some good breaks it is Clark because nobody in my experience has suffered more bad ones. At almost every stage of his life fate has hammered him into the ground and so it is fitting that at last the good things are starting to happen for him.

Life squelched him right at the beginning by separating his parents. He lived with his mother until she died when he was 10 years old and he had to make a fresh start, moving to his father's home in Garforth, Yorkshire.

The tradition introduced him to golf, for his father was a county player and within a year Howard was down to a 12 handicap and improving fast.

He was picked to play for Yorkshire, lost both his matches and was not selected again that season. Squelch. He made the Walker Cup team and played well but the following week suffered humiliating defeat in the first round of the US Amateur championship. Squelch.

He turned pro at 19 and suffered all the normal squelches of tournament golf, many of them, it must be said, compounded by a temperament which insisted that he punish the club for a bad shot by beating it into the turf or, until he went beyond his pain threshold, against his foot.

The problem was that his anger carried over to the next shot and his toughest battle, and greatest victory, has been against that inner demon.

After four years of campaigning he won his place in the Ryder Cup

174

team and practised hard for the match. He was not selected for the opening foursomes and was then informed by a spectator that he had been dropped from the four-balls. Squelch. He was then thrown in as sacrificial lamb against the American lead-off man for the singles, Lanny Wadkins, and duly beaten. Squelch.

In 1978 Clark teamed up with a new caddie, Lawrence Herraty, an American with high academic qualifications in business administration but who preferred the open fairways to the corporate jungle. With his maturity, keen intelligence and understanding nature, Herraty made the perfect counterpoint to Clark's volatility and they formed a winning combination.

For once the plural pronoun would have been justified in the caddies' idiom ('We played well from tee to green but he putted like a dog') although Herraty, almost uniquely among caddies, never insinuated any credit for Clark's success. It was not necessary, being all too obvious.

Two wins and a second place in the space of three weeks brought Clark instant stardom. Ironically, fate was still waiting in the shadows with a sock of wet sand to spoil the triumph. Everything was happening so quickly for Clark that he could not cope with the process of stardom. His game, his marriage and his business involvements went to pot and Herraty went to Australia. Squelch.

Since then Clark has doggedly rehabilitated his life and his game and progressed to the status of one of the world's leading players, confirming that elevation by winning the individual honours in last year's World Cup.

Not everyone saw it that way, however. Clark was not invited to compete in the US Masters and chairman Hord Hardin completed that squelch with a memorable left and right, referring to him as Clive Clark and saying that he had a spotty record.

The Observer, 1985

Moe Norman

The crowd behind the 18th green cheered as the leader's approach shot smacked into the turf. The ball took two hops and then reversed under the effect of backspin, finishing 3 feet from the flag. The leader, now with three strokes for victory, walked briskly on to the green and deliberately clipped the ball into a bunker with his putter.

He splashed the ball back on to the green and, with his usual perfunctory glance along the line, stroked it into the hole.

Can you name the golfer? Well, a bit more of the story. With radio reporters vamping madly and promising to have the winner at the microphone any minute now, and with distraught tournament officials unable to delay the presentation ceremony any longer, the hero of the hour was hiding in a toilet until the hullabaloo died down and he could slip away quietly into the night in his battered old Cadillac.

You may never have heard of him, but mention that incident, or a hundred more like it, to any of the great players in North America and identification will be instantaneous.

'It could only be Moe Norman.' They speak his name with awe, and affection, and amused exasperation, and sometimes with a hint of envy, for Norman is blessed with a talent for striking a golf ball which is as legendary as his eccentricity.

Ever since I first began to hear weird and wonderful tales of Norman I have been trying to track him down but he is a will-of-the-wisp character. Where do you start looking for a man who habitually sleeps in his car, who keeps on the move and is so suspicious of strangers that he refuses to entrust his money to a bank?

Moe drifted into golf the way most boys of his generation did, by hanging around a golf club and earning pocket money as a caddie. The club in question was in Kitchener, Ontario, and Moe was coached by the pro, Lloyd Tucker, who was responsible for bringing on quite a few fine Canadian players.

The one element which Tucker did not drill into Norman was a classical style. All his life Norman has stood to the ball stiff legged, knees braced back, with a pronounced stoop from the waist and with his hands as far from his body as he could get them with fully stretched arms.

176

His impact on Canadian amateur golf was sensational. He would not have a caddy, remarking 'bag's not heavy, bag's not heavy', much to the tight-lipped disapproval of established figures in the Royal Canadian Golf Association. He won everything, Canadian Amateur championships and provincial championships, seemingly as he pleased.

The town of Kitchener turned out in force to hail the local hero at a Moe Norman night, with the full ceremonial of civic speeches, presentation and fanfares. Needless to say Norman did not turn up.

In match-play events he often conceded 10-foot putts – 'that's good, that's good' – and then won the hole by rolling home his 15-footers, a devastating psychological gambit which finally left opponents unable to hole the vital two-footer and which stood him in good stead in his coming career among the rich pigeons.

Lesser amateur tournaments put up the usual prizes such as TV sets, furniture and other household appliances. Norman won four rocking-chair first prizes in successive years. He began to get cute and it was at this time that he learned how to produce the exact score he needed, a facility later to win him many bets as a gypsy pro touring the resort courses down South. He would ask around if anyone wanted to buy a radio for instance, and then, having made the deal and set the price, he would contrive to finish in the place which carried the radio as the prize.

Officialdom frowned on such covert professionalism, drawing from Norman the classic response: 'What do you do with 27 toasters?'

However, Norman was persuaded to do the decent thing and turn pro. He made the Canadian PGA championship virtually a Moe Norman benefit but in other professional events he sometimes seemed completely uninterested.

'Don't know if I want to win. Just a walk in the park, just a walk in the park.'

Eventually Norman was persuaded much against his inclinations to venture into the big pond of the American tour. He was so overawed at first that his main interest was in diffidently asking the star players for their autographs. His friend Bert Turcotte was exasperated: 'Moe, what the hell are you doing? You're out here to whip these guys' asses.'

'Me?' said Norman in astonishment at the idea. 'Oh, no. I'm not supposed to beat them.'

Norman is a Coca-Cola addict and at the Los Angeles Open he walked on to the first tee carrying a bottle, which he placed on the turf. Then, to the delight of the gallery, he put his ball on the top of the bottle and drove off. On another occasion he balanced his ball on a pyramid tee marker and drove off from that. Sometimes, to relieve the tedium of practice rounds, he would throw down a ball and leap into the shot while the ball was still rolling, cracking it 250 yards down the middle.

At Augusta, Norman made history as the only player ever to walk out of the Masters. He had caused something of a stir behind the scenes by sacking the caddie allotted to him before the poor man had even picked up the bag and then, when a breeze blew up for the third round with Norman in fifth position, he said: 'Too windy for golf. Back to Canada, back to Canada,' and disappeared.

Norman and the big time were clearly incompatible and mutually happy to end the association. For one thing it was not too good for the image of professional golf to have a player striking side bets with the gallery, such as whether he could keep a ball bouncing on his club face as he walked along the fairway (his record was 193 bounces) or whether he could get down from a bunker in two strokes with one hand.

For me, Norman's greatest claim to fame lay in one of his favourite sidelines. I have told this story before and repeat it without shame. When opportunity arose, or could be contrived, he would strike a wager that he could break the course record, without even having seen the course. He has collected on 17 such bets to date and on this particular occasion was playing with the local pro. He came to the last needing a four to win his wager and asked the other pro what kind of hole it was. 'Drive and nine-iron,' he was told. Norman took out his nine-iron and hit the ball off the tee, following it with a full driver shot off the fairway to the flag for a birdie three.

If you are ever in Ontario (in summer) or Florida when the snow makes golf impossible in Canada and a scruffy, portly man in his early fifties asks if you would like a game of golf with a little bit of interest on the side, settle for a wager you can well afford to lose and jump at the opportunity. You might just be in for a golf lesson from one of the game's consummate masters.

The Guardian, 1981

Jack Newton

That strong right arm had won 30 amateur titles by the time it thrust an Australian passport at the immigration officer at Heathrow for the first time. It was a specimen arm, developed for the professional purpose of teaching physical education before its owner decided that it might be put to better use winning prize money at golf.

The arm had got Jack Newton into, and out of, enough trouble to fill a lurid novel by the time it slapped me on the back in the late Sixties. Someone, probably Norman von Nida, had told Newton to look me up and that initial contact between the shoulder blades hurtled me towards the bar. The sight of the arm hoisting a pint towards a lopsided grin and a pair of eyes gleaming with devilish mischief was to become part of my life.

The urbane Peter Thomson did not approve of Newton. Thomson saw him as perpetuating the Australian caricature, a cross between Bazza McKenzie and Sir Les Patterson. Certainly it was an ultra-Australian arm, brash, boozey and bawdy, and not much given to reaching for Cicero's Orations from the library shelf. But I cannot think of another right arm in all the world I would sooner have on my side in a tight corner; it was utterly reliable and utterly loyal to its friends.

Occasionally it incurred disapproval, such as the time it felled the president of a continental golf club in mid-tournament, but its good deeds more than made up for the bad. In 1974 it achieved its finest triumph. It was during the old Benson and Hedges matchplay championship at Downfield, Dundee, and the arm was pitted in the semi-final against Neil Coles, then at the peak of his exceptional powers.

I have never seen golf such as the arm produced that day. It took only 13 holes to dispose of Coles by 6 and 5. For those 13 holes the arm was 10 under par, having finished birdie, birdie, eagle, birdie, birdie. Cesar Sanudo did not have a prayer against the arm in the final.

The following year the arm reached out for greatness by finishing in a tie with Tom Watson for the Open championship at Carnoustie. This was one occasion when Newton allowed the playboy mask to slip and he revealed the serious sportsman which he normally kept so closely concealed. He was paired with Jack Nicklaus early in the championship and afterwards he told me that he had just observed the first round of real golf of his life. 'Christ! I've just been playing at this game.' He sat down and spent the next hour analysing every shot that Nicklaus had played, working out why he had taken an iron off certain tees, the reasoning behind his chosen target areas, why he had adjusted the flight of his ball for different shots.

When the arm lost the play-off by a stroke I reached out to give it a consoling hand-shake. 'There's one thing about it,' said Newton, 'at least I didn't choke like one of you poms.'

In due course, Newton decided to chance his arm in America. Like many another golfer who glories in his strength and hits flat out, he had injury problems. For months he had to wear a medical contraption like an old-fashioned truss on that strong right arm to contain muscular damage but it did not slow him down noticeably.

At the Canadian Open I had occasion to put my head round the doorway of the bar of my hotel, probably to check my watch against the wall clock, or some equally innocent reason.

Like all such bars it was dimly lit and from the gloom I heard a familiar rasping voice: 'It's your shout, you bastard.' That was the night of the first Leonard-Duran fight and, true to his bull-like nature, Newton insisted that Duran would walk it. That turned into a big night. In boxing, the correct way to counter an onrushing bull is to play the matador but for some reason Leonard chose to adopt the role of the china shop and the arm gleefully pocketed a pom 10 dollar note.

The arm's talents were not confined to golf. It is impossible for a specialist in one sport to make pronouncements about other games, not that we are inhibited from doing so, but respected judges have said that Newton could have made it to the top as a cricketer. He certainly had success as a junior and he was the backbone of the professional golfers' cricket team. We used to play beer matches in Essex against Pleshey on the village green and the arm opened with both bat and ball. As wicket keeper I used to station myself on the boundary and take him on the first bounce. Lord knows how many balls we lost among the sugar beet when he went in to bat.

In Zambia, the arm was called into novel service when Newton was sizing up a short chip shot to the 17th green in the last round of the Cock o' the North tournament. As he stood in deep concentration, an army of soldier ants proceeded in columns of twos up his trouser leg. The words which were uttered should not properly be heard during the gentlemanly game of golf but on this one occasion were possibly excusable.

Newton put a safe distance between himself and the advancing support columns and the arm slapped wildly at his person, to no effect against the armour-plated invaders.

There was nothing else for it. The arm tore every shred of clothing off his body and he and his wife, Jackie, counter attacked against the ants which by now were digging in and diving for whatever cover they could find. Between them, the Newtons finally picked off the last survivors and I have always regarded Newton's victory in that tournament as his finest achievement.

Now the whirring propeller of a Cessna at Sydney airport has sheared off that mighty arm. In everyday speech, we often say that we would give our right arms to achieve some objective. The opportunity is not available, of course, and talk is cheap, but I would have made a considerable sacrifice to have that hell-raising right arm reunited in full working order.

It is difficult to imagine Newton without the arm and my first reaction was that without the best part of him he would only be half the man he was. That is sentimental drivel, of course. The best part of Jack Newton is his devil-may-care zest for life and that will come through unscathed. He could out-drink and out-fight most men with one arm tied behind his back and if that is the way it has to be in future then, if anybody can handle it, Newton can and will.

The Observer, 1983

Ballesteros revisited ————

It may not be the most elegant of expressions, and perhaps we should not inquire too deeply into its origins, but there is nothing Severiano Ballesteros likes better than sticking it to them.

He is hypersensitive to a slight or injury and cherishes his grudges like a miser gloating over his hoard of gold pieces. People, places, golf courses, events and even entire nations which incur his displeasure are marked down for vengeance. It may take years but eventually he will stick it to them. He is not content just to even up the score, he needs to win the replay 10 and 8.

When he first became a tournament professional Ballesteros was poor and money was motivation enough. He very soon acquired enough money to turn it into an irrelevant abstraction and he had to find a new fuel to drive him to the limits of his endeavours. Sticking it to them was the answer.

The European circuit angered him by trying to ban appearance money, a move which he interpreted, with some justification, as an act of victimisation against him personally, and he stuck it to the circuit by resigning and boycotting European tournaments.

He became dissatisfied with the service he was getting from his American manager, Ed Barner, and stuck it to him by refusing to renew his contract, following the example of previous Barner clients, Billy Casper and Johnny Miller.

He was irked by American players and writers calling him lucky when he won the Open championship at Lytham and he stuck it to them by winning their precious Masters tournament. Almost any other player in the world would have taken a week's rest after winning a major championship, but Ballesteros was chafing at what he considered to be less than his due recognition by the Spanish press and sporting public. He flew straight to the Madrid Open and stuck it to them by winning.

The United States Open championship, the United States Golf Association and, by extension, the entire North American continent incurred his resentment because of his humiliating disqualification for late arrival on the tee at Baltusrol in 1981, even though it was entirely his own fault as he freely admits. Nevertheless it was necessary for him to stick it to America, which he did in fine style by winning another Masters.

It would have been even more satisfactory to have stuck it to the USGA by winning the Open at Oakmont last week but that was not to be and the championship must be carried forward for further treatment. Actually if you wanted to set out deliberately to stop Ballesteros winning a tournament you could do no better than to set up the course according to the USGA's specification for their Open.

Even so, by superbly disciplined play against all his natural inclinations, he almost made it. Every champion needs a few breaks but nothing went for him in the last round and he had to settle for fourth place. On the other hand everything went in favour of Larry Nelson in the final 36 holes. It was a timely triumph because it ended an extremely lean spell for Nelson, whose ability was surely misrepresented by a career record of only four tournament victories and one previous major championship, the 1981 American PGA.

The excellent win by Ballesteros in the previous week's West-chester Classic is probably best interpreted as not so much a sticking of it to America as to Deane Beman, the commissioner of the American tour. For a long time Ballesteros has wanted to play more American tournaments provided that he can also fulfil his contractual obligations, and also his loyalties, to the European tour. The American tour has a rule that foreign players can obtain automatic releases to play on their home circuits. Ballesteros argues that this rule should be interpreted in his case to mean Europe; Beman insists that automatic releases would be limited to tournaments in Spain. My bet is that Ballesteros will win that argument by continuing to stick it to the US tour through such stratagems as winning the American PGA championship in August and then boycotting the World Series.

In the meantime Ballesteros has two more outstanding victims overdue for having him stick it to them. In the case of the Ryder Cup he may be in the mood for an exciting double thrust. The PGA has it coming to them for their petty-mindedness in not selecting him for the 1981 team. On the other hand the American team has it coming to them in retribution for Ballesteros's failure to gain a single point in the 1979 match.

The other culprit is Royal Birkdale Golf Club, where one error of judgment cost Ballesteros the Open championship of 1976. In a month's time Ballesteros has his opportunity to release seven years of accumulated resentment against those mighty links. I can hardly wait to see him stick it to Birkdale.

The Observer, 1983

Brian Mayo

On a rainy Tuesday in October, 1979, Brian Mayo played in a South Wales Alliance golf meeting in Glamorganshire. He played rather well, as he had four days previously when he had come within one stroke of winning the championship of his home club at Maes y Cwmmer, on the Gwent border. In short, he was just another golfing fanatic taking a day off to indulge his passion.

That passion for golf had prompted him to join forces with three partners, all connected with the building trade, to buy the run-down 100-acre hill farm of Bedwas Uchas, consisting of 34 pocket handkerchief fields and the ruins of the 600-year-old farm buildings of traditional design; ground floor for cattle and pigs and dwellings upstairs for the farmer and his family.

Inspired by the spectacular views across Islwyn and working 15 hours a day, the partners had created Bryn Meadows golf and country club, a short and sporty 18-holer of 6,140 yards, par-71, and an elegant clubhouse with the pigsty converted to a billiard room and the cows' quarters transformed into the dining room.

More of Bryn Meadows later. For the moment let us return to that Alliance meeting and Brian Mayo whose name, like that of so many Welsh families, derives from the human flotsam which survived the wreckage of the Spanish armada. Like many keen golfers he was meticulous about keeping his ball shining clean and had developed the habit of giving it a lick and polishing it on his sweater. The course had just been dressed with fertiliser and treated with weed killer.

That evening he experienced a feeling of drowsiness which persisted for the next three days. He kept falling asleep. On the Friday of that week he changed into his dinner jacket for the annual dinner of the Gwent Golf Union, deciding even as he did so that he felt altogether too seedy to attend. The last thing he recalls is looking at the clock, which read 7.15 p.m.

He regained consciousness three weeks later in the intensive care unit of Royal Gwent Hospital, Newport. It was 5.15 in the morning and his family were assembled at his bedside: wife Fay, Stephen, 16 and Gary, 11. They had been urgently summoned to take leave of a 43-year-old husband and father they could barely recognise, reduced from a strapping 11 stone to a skeletal 98 pounds. He could scarcely see them because his sight was impaired by a rare form of meningitis, the first known case since the fatality of a woman in Holland in 1952, induced by a toxic substance he had licked from his golf ball.

How he survived Brian Mayo does not know, but he is convinced that he owes his life to the lucky chance of being admitted to the hospital served by Dr I.S. Petheram. Fay Mayo concurs with that opinion. She had told the hospital that she wanted the best man in this field that money could buy and had been told: 'Don't worry, you've already got him.'

That November Mayo was transferred to Chepstow Hospital where his legs, black and hard as boards, were plastered together, with the circulatory system of his right leg channelled through his decomposing left foot. Some flesh regenerated and formed a healthy skin cover but now the sole of his left foot turned septic. Brian Mayo felt ashamed of his helplessness and pathetically grateful to the nurse who had to cope with his helplessness for six weeks.

He was on a rich diet to build him up and a massive daily regime of pills, with no idea of what was happening to him and totally unprepared for what came next. The doctor said matter of factly: 'If I were you I would have both legs amputated.'

Brian Mayo pulled the sheet over his head, determined to count up to 10 to quell his panic. By the time he reached seven he had come to terms with the medical verdict.

His left leg was amputated below the knee on Christmas Eve, the right leg being removed in May 1980. Between the two operations he read *Reach for the Sky*, the story of the legless Battle of Britain ace, Douglas Bader, and thought: 'If he could do it I can at least try.' Dickie Henderson was a regular and encouraging visitor at his bedside.

He was fitted with artificial legs and the first thing he did on returning home was to fix up scaffolding handrails to teach himself to walk. He progressed to walking with sticks. Then, as he was exercising, he heard a favourite piece of music on the radio. Something in the rhythm triggered his reflexes and he threw away the sticks.

Six weeks after getting his artificial legs he was visited by a cousin from Norfolk, John Jones. The two men drove to St Pierre, Chepstow, the nearest golf club which had motorised carts. 'On the way I was as excited as a child going off on his first school treat.' He played 18 holes, quickly adjusting to the fact that without legs the ball had to be struck with a pure swing. He made par on one hole.

Mayo and another club golfer, David Alexander, partnered Henry Cooper in Jimmy Tarbuck's celebrity-amateur charity tournament at Wallasey and they won it. His personal score was 84. He almost won another tournament, the annual meeting of golf club secretaries at Hoylake, but spoiled his chance by driving out of bounds at the 16th. These days Mayo is winning rather often.

Shortly after returning from hospital he had bought out his partner's interests in Bryn Meadows and it is now run as a family concern with, as he drily puts it, his sons doing the leg work.

Planning permission has been granted for a 20-bedroom hotel at the club, and a swimming pool. But first he has a date at the Albert Hall on Thursday for the Douglas Bader Awards ceremonies. 'He was an inspiration to us all,' says Brian Mayo, who himself is a bit of a lesson and an inspiration to all of us golfers, even if he is a bandit off eleven. Legs eleven. Tin legs eleven.

The Observer, 1981

Tom Watson

Tom Watson is the world's leading golfer. He is also the world's leading golf perfectionist. In order to get some inkling of what that means it is necessary to understand a little of what is required to drive a golf ball down a fairway. Having raised his club, the golfer must complete the following precise sequence:

For the first $^{17}/_{100}$ sec in the downward movement he must apply a pull on the club which increases smoothly from 2lb to 6lb; in the next $^{15}/_{100}$ sec that pull must increase explosively to 70lb and then drop to zero in the last $^{4}/_{100}$ sec before impact.

This surge of energy, amounting to 1.45 horse power, accelerates the 7½oz club-head through centrifugal force from zero to 166 feet per second. The club-head, which now 'weighs' 110lb in pull directly down the shaft, strikes the ball with an impact of 1½ tons. The force of impact compresses the ball on the club-face, distorting it to about two-thirds of its normal diameter of 1.68in. Contact is maintained for $^{4}/_{10,000}$ sec over travel of $^{2}/_{3}$in, with the ball skidding up the club-face 1 millimetre, and then taking up a reverse rotation as the compressed elasticity is released and the ball is despatched at 225 feet per second. Under those forces, average for a good professional, the ball travels about 280 yards.

Of course, it may not go in a straight line. The criteria for a straight shot are that the club-head must meet the ball along the target line (a 2 degree error will send it into the rough); the centre of mass of the club-head must meet the target axis of the ball within a tolerance of $^{3}/_{8}$in or the force will be dissipated; the face of the club must be square to the target line (a 3 degree error will impart enough sidespin to slice or hook the ball into the rough); and the angle of attack of club-face to ball must be within these same exacting limits.

Several scientists who have set out to analyse the game of golf have concluded in all seriousness that it is impossible for a human being to combine such degrees of power, timing and accuracy within these precise margins.

Watson has devoted much of his life to the proposition that it is not only possible to achieve these criteria every time he swings a club but that these tolerances can be refined even further. He has an obsession to conquer the game.

All professional golfers want to improve, it goes without saying, in order to further their ambitions. In most cases that means to acquire as much money as possible. In rarer cases the motivation is to accumulate major titles and establish themselves as giants in the annals of golf. Jack Nicklaus is the supreme example of a golfer who is spurred to secure unassailable credentials as the greatest golfer who ever lived.

Watson is chasing self-satisfaction. His aim is domination of that 1.62oz white sphere to the point where he can manoeuvre it at will, high or low, flighting to the left or right, with such perfect precision that it will land within feet of his chosen target some 200-odd yards distant and still retain control of the ball's bounce and roll after it has pitched into the turf.

His quest is hopeless, of course. There are too many variables beyond the player's control to achieve theoretical perfection. A golfer can judge the effect on a shot of wind strength and direction but once the ball is in the air it is at the mercy of capricious gusts. It is impossible to judge precisely what the compression of grass between club-face and ball will do to alter the distance and trajectory of a shot. Golf balls themselves vary one from another, in symmetry and surface imperfections.

The texture of the landing area is another imponderable, since it may be soft or hard and the golfer unable to tell which. Humidity and barometric pressure affect the behaviour of the ball, as do changing biological balances within the golfer from shot to shot. The best the golfer can do is to make an intelligent guess about these variables and then make a perfect contact.

Ben Hogan, the ultimate perfectionist as a striker before Watson came along, devoted his life to refining his technique. By common consent he got closer than anyone to mechanical precision and at the peak of his powers Hogan reckoned that he hit no more than two shots exactly the way he wanted in any round of golf.

These two men, who grappled with the intricacies of golf technique for its own sake rather than as a means to an end, could hardly be more different. Hogan was the son of a blacksmith whose ill health and inability to find work in the depression drove him to take his life at the age of 37, when Hogan was nine. It took Hogan 18 years to fight (sometimes literally) his way to security in golf, through the ranks of the caddies and years of desperate privation as tournament gypsy.

Watson came from middle class, middle America and had all the advantages of a middle class education – private schooling and Stanford University, where he graduated in psychology and played golf. He was a typical heir to the American dream and everyone, himself included, assumed that he would go into the family chemical business, settle down to marriage with his childhood sweetheart in a desirable suburb of Kansas, and start the whole cycle over again with a brood of heirs to that American dream. Watson's nearest and dearest were less than ecstatic when, late in his college career, he decided to make golf his profession.

Perhaps vocation is a better word because Watson had no yearning for fame (he is still uncomfortable in his role of celebrity and hates being lionised) and no lust for money. He thus joined the most ruthless free-for-all in world sport with neither of the motivating forces normally considered to be essential for survival.

Watson survived because he had his personal challenge with the golf swing to spur him through endless hours on the practice ground. His obsession is a priceless asset because it allows him to play golf for its own sake, without the destructive pressures which afflict the hungry and the ambitious. He just about covered his expenses in his first year, did rather better than that the second season, but he still had not won a tournament when he played himself into a potentially winning position in the US Open championship at Winged Foot in 1974.

It is almost axiomatic in golf that nobody succeeds at the first attempt. Everything has to be learned from painful experience, and that includes the technique of winning, which requires balance between aggression and caution, control of nerves and judgment under exceptional emotional pressures, and marshalling of rebellious physical and mental resources. Watson, a stranger to this turmoil, scored a last round 79 and was instantly labelled a 'choker'. The cruel tag stuck as Watson fell out of contention again in the US Open the following year and in several regular tournaments.

By this time he was winning tournaments but when he was pipped at the post it was assumed that he had simply blown it again, or lost his bottle. The best golfers do not play themselves into a winning position every week, by any means. On those occasions when a golfer is in contention after three rounds, he is doing exceptionally well if he wins one tournament in three. Watson was achieving that level of success by the time he played the 1977 Masters, that great golfing classic at Augusta, Georgia. Towards the end of the last round there were only two players in it, Watson and Jack Nicklaus. Watson won by a stroke and finally shrugged off that choker label.

British golf fans could not understand how the calumny had ever started. In the 1975 Open championship at Carnoustie, Watson showed no frailties in winning a tense play-off against Jack Newton, nor in his Ryder Cup matches two years later. And again in 1977, during a historic week at Turnberry, Watson proved himself to be a man with nerves of tungsten. He and Nicklaus were paired together for the last two rounds. Nicklaus, the most formidable golfer the world has known, kept seizing an advantage of one, two or even three holes. Every time Nicklaus went ahead Watson clawed his way back on to level terms. On the 71st hole Nicklaus faltered and the fresh-faced kid from Kansas had his freckled nose in front. By a titanic effort of will Nicklaus salvaged a birdie from the wreckage of a poor drive at the last hole. Watson topped it with an impeccably played birdie of his own.

That week Watson had a glimpse of his goal of golfing mastery. He has expressed his ambition like this: 'I am waiting for the day when everything falls into place, everthing makes sense, when every swing is with confidence and every shot is exactly what I want.

'I know it can be done. I've been close enough to smell it a couple of times, but I'd like to touch it, to feel it. I know it's been touched. Hogan touched it. Bryan Nelson touched it. I want to touch it. Then I think I would be satisfied. Then, I think, I could walk away from the game.'

Watson certainly smelled it on the last hole at Turnberry and the records show that he is getting closer. He has been the number one golfer in America (which means the world, in effect) for the past three years.

That is not to say that he is the best player every week, nor that he will walk away with the championship at Muirfield this week. He is subject to the normal fluctuations of form, which appear rather more pronounced in his case because of his Charge of the Light Brigade approach to golf.

Most professionals can fiddle their way round in respectable figures when they lose their edge. The only way Watson knows to play the game is to go for the flag, a philosophy shared by the prodigious Spaniard Severiano Ballesteros. Golf courses are arranged so that such shots, unless executed perfectly, are punished most severely. When Watson is off his stick his scores zoom up to the 78/79 levels, but when he is sniffing close on the scent of that elusive quarry his golf is sublime. It happens about six times a year.

Will he ever fully achieve his ambition and hit every shot exactly the way he wants? The quest seems hopeless. Hogan did not come close to it. For one summer Byron Nelson approached nearer to it than anyone and the strain broke him; after winning 18 tournaments in that one year he was physically sick and his nerve could not take any more. Watson might well surpass them both, possibly to the point of hitting one perfect shot in five. If he could achieve such a level of performance he would indeed be the greatest golfer of them all. But the world would not recognise him as such, because golfers are judged by their accumulation of victories and, at 30, he does not have enough time left to crack the records. It is just as well that self-satisfaction will be reward enough for him. I hope he gets close enough to his impossible dream to enjoy his private triumph, for in his searchings along the way he has given enormous satisfaction to millions.

Observer colour magazine, 1980

Faldo and the demon

Rudyard Kipling didn't have much time for golf. Polo and pig sticking were more in his line. It was all the more remarkable, then, that he was able to predict so accurately what was going to happen to the European Tour 100 years later. He even anticipated that golfers would call themselves by the names of animals, great white shark, golden bear and so on, and he therefore used a jungle metaphor for his uncanny prophecy.

You remember his story of How The Elephant Got Its Trunk, of course. Originally all elephants had normal noses not a whit bigger than say, Barry Manilow's. This young elephant, who was much put upon by the bullying adults, went down to the river for a drink and a crocodile grabbed him by the hooter. The beasts of the jungle raced to his rescue and pulled him from behind, the tug o' war ending with rescue for the young elephant who by now had a greatly extended proboscis. Armed with this prehensile appendage, the young elephant returned to the herd and whaled the tar out of his tormentors who in self defence had to go to the river for nose jobs from the crocodile.

In this prophetic parable we have the life story of Nick Faldo, today the dominant leader of the golfing herd while his hapless rivals go trooping off to Florida to get the crocodile treatment from David Leadbetter. But will they have the character, the patience and the sheer guts which Faldo displayed during the long and painful process of acquiring his trunk?

He is a much misunderstood man. But the key to his character is that he is possessed of a demon, the Demon of Ambition.

In this he is in the historic tradition of golfing champions going back to William St Clair of Roslyn, winner of the silver clubs of St Andrews and the Honourable Company of Edinburgh Golfers back in the 18th century. This remarkable character, whose red-coated figure is celebrated in one of the most reproduced golfing prints of all time, was so skilled at golf and archery that he was thought to have sold his soul to a witch.

Every great player since then has been the subject of demonic possession, none more so than Jack Nicklaus. These are men apart and they deserve some effort from us to understand, and therefore forgive, them. Allowances must be made for the behaviour of people who are consumed by an obsession because it is that obsession which makes them heroes. I remember Faldo playing in the grandiosely-titled World Under-25 Championship in France when his ball became entangled in some tree roots. At the end of the round he flipped his card, unsigned, into the recorder's caravan and ran into the clubhouse to pack his gear.

Consternation gripped the sponsor who was about to lose the only name player in the field from disqualification, as decreed by the committee. My counsel was beseeched and I pointed out that the committee had power to waive disqualification in exceptional circumstances. What is exceptional, they asked me, about an angry brat refusing to sign his scorecard? He is exceptional, I replied. At that moment he was physically incapable of putting his signature to such a card. Try him now that he has had a chance to cool down. Faldo was duly persuaded to sign the card and continue the tournament, but I was glad he never knew who was responsible for delaying his return home.

In those days he had a long overswing and a tremendous willowy hip slide, a typically young man's action which propelled the ball enormous distances, not always in the desired direction. He was good enough to win at least one tournament a year from the time he turned pro as a teenager and to walk straight into the Ryder Cup team, beating Tom Watson in his single and winning both foursomes and fourballs in partnership with Peter Oosterhuis.

In 1983 he won five tournaments and was ranked European No. 1, progress that most players would have regarded as highly satisfactory. Not Faldo. In several Open championships he played himself right into contention but his game did not stand up to the crunch of the last nine holes. He determined that he must achieve consistency, no matter what it might take.

It took two years out of his golfing life with nary a sniff of victory. It took a massive drop in his income. It took an agony of frustration, grinding hard work, and the pain of Leadbetter's incisors clamped to his nose. It took the embarrassment of the bewildered criticism of his golfing colleagues and many others who understood even less about demonology.

Slowly the metamorphosis was achieved. Faldo emerged with a shorter, flatter, controlled swing which did not break down under pressure. Nobody kept the ball in play better than Faldo during the storms of the 1987 Open at Muirfield and the critics who labelled his winning final round of 18 straight pars as "dull" merely exposed their ignorance of golf.

Walter Hagen declared that anyone can win one major; you are not a real champion until you repeat. Faldo repeated in quick order: 1989 US Masters, 1990 US Masters, 1990 Open championship. He was frustrated in his bid to equal Ben Hogan's record of three major championships in one year because the American PGA championship was played on a freaky golf course prepared in a freaky condition. At Shoal Creek the punishment did not remotely fit the crime, the sanction for minor misdemeanors being savage sentences. The players were denied the opportunity to redeem their slight errors with the skills of their recovery play. It was a test unworthy of a major championship. (N.B. this is a personal assessment and does not necessarily represent the official view of the publisher who is highly diplomatic and anxious to maintain good fraternal relations with all golfing associations).

No matter. It is a subject of some embarrassment to me as a member of the advisory committee of the Sony World Rankings that Faldo's two major championships in 1990 did not instantly propel him above Greg Norman into the No. 1 spot. The formula is not designed to reflect a player's current form. After all, Hale Irwin was the best golfer in the world during the week of the US Open, ahead of Mike Donald, but it would have been absurd for them to be ranked in first and second place.

The world rankings are determined over a rolling four-year period and therefore represent a broader assessment of a player's standing in the pecking order of golf. Even so, I acknowledge, along with everyone else, that Faldo is now Numero Uno and nothing that I have seen lately challenges my belief that he will remain the world's dominant player for years to come.

Success and security seem on the surface to have changed Faldo's personality. He appears more assured, more congenial, more tolerant and appreciative of the need to live up to the standards of a champion. Many people have remarked that he is a much nicer guy these days. Actually, he has always been a nice guy. It is just that these days he manages to hide the torment he is suffering from his inner demon and we do not see outbursts of petulance any more.

That's fine, just so long as the demon is still in there jabbing at his vitals with a pitchfork. After all, without his demon Faldo would be just another golfer.

Volvo PGA championship programme, 1991

Chapter 8

In the past tense, alas

Eric Brown

Ignore a man's faults and you eviscerate him. Eric Brown would have hated to be represented solely by his good qualities because such a portrait would be hypocritical and insipid, an impression which he would have found both ludicrous and insulting.

His whole bearing and manner proclaimed a challenge: this is the way I am, take it or leave it. If you don't care for what you see, then bugger off. It's all the same to me.

Hard, arrogant, opinionated, bloody-minded, proud, outspoken, fiery tempered – at times he was all of these and on occasion the combination, particularly when inflamed by booze, made him virtually unplayable. But flip the coin and those faults had their complementary virtues in full measure: manliness, honesty, a fierce loyalty as a friend and husband, a refreshing zest for life, an unquenchable fighting spirit and a capacity for finding amusement from unlikely circumstances.

Supplemented by a fine talent those virtues made him a terrific player. The faults surely prevented him from fulfilling his potential as a great champion.

One round of golf sums up Eric Brown as a player. In the second round of the Dunlop Masters of 1955 at Little Aston, Brown's superb play had him six under par for 11 holes. He was a mighty driver in those days and his one weakness was that about twice a round he would spray a tee shot.

Even though he went with his three-wood from the 12th tee in order to play short of the cross bunkers he pulled his ball into thick rough which was flattened and soaked by rain, the kind of wrist-breaking, clinging lie which ought to be eliminated from the face of the earth. The prudent course would have been to hack the ball sideways, to regain the fairway at all costs. That was never Brown's style. He took a straight-faced club and went for the flag. He moved the ball a few inches, burying it deeper into the wiry tangle. The hot blood rose in him and swamped his judgment. He took another slash. And another. And another. He needed eight furious hacks to get the ball on to the fairway and then, with a certain inevitability, played his next shot into a bunker by the green. The hole cost him a 12.

But that temper, which he always insisted was quick rather than bad, subsided into a wry laugh and he went back to work. He scored 73, quite possibly a tournament record for a card with a 12 on it.

Brown was a boy prodigy, winning the West Lothian Boys

championship at 13 and going on to further success. In Scotland they know about the uncertainties of precocious talent and Brown took a job with the railways so that he would have a career to fall back on if golf failed him. However, when he won the Scottish Amateur championship at Carnoustie, he felt confident enough to turn pro. In those days you had to serve a five-year apprenticeship before you could play PGA tournaments so Brown sought experience on the Continent.

It was a good grounding for a young golfer, with strong competition from Bobby Locke, Flory van Donck, Henry Cotton, Dai Rees, Fred Daly and Charlie Ward. Brown proved that he could live in this company, winning the Open championships of Switzerland, Italy, Portugal and Ireland.

By the time he had served his apprenticeship he was a hardened competitor and immediately became a major force on the PGA tournament circuit. He went on to win 20 or so major tournaments, represented Scotland 12 times in the World Cup, took innumerable regional titles in Scotland, played four Ryder Cup matches winning his singles on each occasion, was appointed captain of the PGA and then captain of two successive Ryder Cup teams, leading his side to a tie at Royal Birkdale in 1969 and the best British and Irish performance to date at St Louis two years later.

In the famous 1957 Ryder Cup match at Lindrick the captain Dai Rees chose Brown to spearhead the counter-attack in the singles, correctly guessing that America's best player, Tommy Bolt, would be played at No. 1. It was a dour, snarling encounter between two men who both saw the event in terms of total awe. Brown won easily and the peppery Bolt growled that he could not say that he had enjoyed the match. The Scot, the quickest verbal counter puncher in golf, snapped back: 'That's because you don't like getting beat.'

The 1959 Open championship at Muirfield was the turning point in Brown's career. He had to withdraw because of a troublesome disc and, although it responded to treatment, Brown was dismayed to find that he had lost considerable length. Golf became a struggle because of the extra pressure on his approach shots and short game. He who had once been the most aggressive, and effective, putter in Britain became nervous and defensive on the greens.

He went on playing, because that was all he knew, but at 43 he had to face the bleak truth that he must look elsewhere to make a living. And he was not suited to the life of a club pro. His reputation brought him appointments but none of them lasted. A brewer gave him charge of a pub, which was like putting a pyromaniac in charge of the fire station. His wife, Joan, fell seriously ill and he himself had problems with his health.

The low point came when he was financially strapped and defaulted on his subscription to the Scottish PGA. The hard drinking, two-fisted element in Scottish life came into conflict with the opposite extreme of lip pursing, shawl-hugging, sanctimonious defenders of moral rectitude, and they were out to make an example of Eric Brown.

Goodness knows, there were faults on both sides, and Brown was always his own worst enemy, but he felt that they wanted him to grovel. That he would not do, nor would he allow proxy grovelling by accepting the many offers from friends to pay off his arrears. So the profession which he had so richly ornamented finally spurned him when what he most needed was help.

When he retired from competitive play, Brown consoled himself with the reflection that the game was becoming so serious that all the fun and the characters had gone out of it.

For those who knew Eric Brown some of the fun and a remarkable character has gone out of our lives.

The Observer, 1988

Leonard Crawley ——————

The first time I covered the US Masters, I was put up at the home of an Augusta member and I was awakened by the noise of drawers being opened by, as I noticed, a burly figure in a dressing-gown who was systematically rifling the room.

Seeing that I was awake, he barked: 'Crawley. Looking for headed notepaper.' At this point he discovered some in a desk. 'Capital. I will give you a copy at breakfast.'

Sure enough, by my plate was a carbon copy of a badly typed note which read: 'To six days' accommodation – 500 dollars'. As a receipt it would not have fooled a newspaper accountant for a minute, but I was touched by the generosity of the gesture.

Leonard Crawley himself was hidden behind the *Augusta Chronicle*. 'Ah-ha,' he announced. 'This chap seems to have a lot of facts. It will do nicely for *The Telegraph*.' So saying, he tore the article

197

from the paper and later in the press room handed it to the secretary he had engaged for the week (that really impressed me) and told her to dictate it to London.

Those first impressions of an engaging scoundrel never totally vanished, but the Leonard Crawley I came to know was a giant. He came into the world through the gentleman's gate, via Harrow and Cambridge, and in those days a triple blue was entitled to assume that life was one long house-party.

His year was ordained by sport. Golf up to the Amateur championship, played in May at that time, then cricket during the summer until the time came to put down the bat and pick up the gun. Crawley excelled at both sports, to the point that at one time he had to decide between playing top in the Walker Cup match or joining Gubby Allen's team on the 1936 Australian tour.

As a golf writer Crawley had a remarkable facility for encapsulating a golfer's style in a vivid and succinct phrase, for he was one of the most astute analysts and teachers of golf I have met, but the *Daily Telegraph* wanted him to write blow by blow reports and that did not suit him at all.

He seldom stayed to the end of a tournament, for there were always birds to be shot on Lord Derby's estate, or gundogs to be delivered somewhere, and the rest of us would cover for him. 'I've sent them a piece but just top it up at the end of play for me. You know the kind of stuff they like.' Perhaps it was best that way for he once reported a match in the Amateur championship between two players, one of whom had been knocked out in an earlier round.

His expenses suffered from the same lack of factual base and for years whenever he was sent abroad, even to France, the first item read: 'To two tropical suits . . .'. *The Telegraph* was not fooled for a minute but happily paid up, maintaining a balance by keeping his salary to a pittance.

One item stretched the Sports Editor's gullibility too far – £25 for entertaining at the Boys' championship. Crawley shrugged aside the objection with lordly disdain: 'It is astonishing how much lemonade the little buggers can get through.'

Leonard Crawley, a name certainly to be mentioned in the same breath as C.B. Fry, died at the age of 77 and the game of golf lost a remarkable player and a well-loved link with Edwardian eccentricity.

The Guardian, 1982

Gerald Micklem

An era in golf ended last weekend with the death at the age of 77 of Gerald Micklem, the game's only authentic oracle on this side of the Atlantic although his friend and counterpart in America, Joe Dey, happily remains with us.

This is not to say that the two men operated like territorial animals, confining their oracular operations to their own spheres of influence. Dey was elected captain of the Royal and Ancient Club of St Andrews, as Micklem had been, and the name 'Gerald' was like a password all over the world.

For 40 years or so anyone who was anyone in golf knew, or knew of, this legendary figure. Very, very few of them ever came close to a passable impersonation of his speech, let alone his acid wit. The plummy Eton and Christnose vowels, actually Winchester and Trinity, were compressed into a Brigade of Guards bark and delivered at high pitch and even higher speed, as they had to be to keep pace with his fertile intellect.

When he made a speech on receiving the Donald Ross award from the American Society of Golf Course Architects the company rose for an ovation and my neighbour remarked: 'That was absolutely fabulous; I didn't understand a single word he said.'

In one sense Gerald was a golfing archetype of his time and class. His Oxford blue gave him entree into the City which in turn enabled him to pursue an active amateur career as an English international, Walker Cup regular and twice English champion. Some care must be taken in assessing his stature as a player because he loathed sycophancy and would have hated the idea of having it laid on too thickly when he was no longer able to administer an astringent corrective.

For a quarter of a century I have stiffened to the Caterham Barracks yelp of 'Golf writer! Git it wrong again on Sunday.' He then put me right on a point of fact or interpretation and, to my shame, it was some time before I penetrated the layers of tribal camouflage with which this breed of Englishman conceals his feelings and realised that he was motivated by a genuine spirit of helpfulness.

Years later, when I had learnt how to read his conversational wrong 'un and understood that kindness and generosity were the keys to his character, I asked him if he would read the manuscript of a book I had written (*Golf Rules Explained*, seventh edition hot off the presses, order now while stocks last).

All my publisher wanted, as Gerald well understood, was the Micklem imprimatur as former chairman of the Rules of Golf committee. He went through the MS word by word and his forthright marginal notations were so revealing that I had to do an extensive rewrite.

So there must be no sloppy hyperbole in assessing Gerald's golf. He himself would probably have settled for some throwaway expression such as 'a pretty useful performer on his day' but he had to be better than that when he won the English in 1953, beating Ronnie White, whom Arnold Palmer reckons the best amateur he has seen.

We are on surer ground in measuring Gerald when he reached the stage of social golf and annual competitive flings in the Oxford and Cambridge Society's competition for the President's Putter, retired from the Stock Exchange and devoted his life to administration.

By the conventions of his background he should have become an Establishment figure, a committee time server inheriting the high offices of the game on the basis of Buggins' turn and gradually declining into the state of pompous old buffer, or elder statesman as it is more politely known.

Publicly he played that part but behind the scenes – and he was behind all the golf scenes – he was a maverick. Golf administration in those days was like a committee meeting of the Athenaeum, life being ordered along the unchanging lines that had been followed for a hundred years. The radical Micklem challenged the established ways, bringing two novel attributes to the discussion: a social conscience and a keen business mind.

Representative teams were selected from chaps of good family and the swankier public schools. Gerald wanted the best golfers and brought in working-class players, covertly buying Ronnie Shade a dinner jacket to dampen the shock waves agitating the reactionaries.

The Open championship was in serious decline. Gerald revitalised it and set it on a business-like footing so that profits could be reinvested into even better championships which attracted all the world's best.

The rules were a legalistic hotch-potch fully understood only by a handful of specialists. Gerald initiated the continuing process of rationalising and reviewing them and wrote a booklet, 'Help in the Interpretation of the Rules', which has become a standard work for the bewildered.

He himself would disclaim personal responsibility for those achievements, pointing out that the game was run by committees of which he was one member, but everyone knew that he supplied the ideas and provided the irresistible dynamic which quelled all opposition.

For these reforms he was awarded the CBE, an inadequate reward in the view of those who understood the magnitude of his contribution, but those were possibly the least of his legacies.

Privately he became a major patron, always concealing his generosity by stealth, which makes it impossible to quantify the amount of good he spread about within the game. But there can be few worthy young amateurs during his time who were not helped, directly or indirectly, by his conviction that poverty should not disqualify a youngster from competing in amateur golf. Ironically, his official status meant that he had to defend and uphold the rigid rules of amateur status in public while privately he dissipated his fortune in breach of it.

There can have been few more avid spectators of golf than Gerald. Until he was grounded by a debilitating illness he devoted the major part of his time to travelling to championships, amateur and professional, and tirelessly walking the course, always with a purpose. He wanted to see how Green would tackle a stretch of holes, whether a tendency to hook under pressure would betray Brown at the water hole, whether Black's new grip was bedding down.

Life will never be the same again without the oracle to whom we could turn for the definitive word on the great issues of golf.

The Observer, 1988

Jack Statter _____

If the Beatitudes are to be trusted, Jack Statter saw God last weekend. The purest and biggest heart you could hope to meet stopped beating early last Sunday morning. Fleet Street died a litle bit, too. So did golf.

Jack was not an important and successful man in the terms by which the world measures these things. In the winter, he worked as a sub-editor for the *Sun* newspaper in a key job which demands a thorough knowledge of editorial and mechanical functions. He acted as the liaison between two highly skilled processes which turn words

and pictures into hot metal and deliver them to the presses on time
and was the best in the business.

In summer, he went free range as golf correspondent for the *Sun*
and created engaging mayhem wherever he went. The war was both
the making and breaking of Jack. It saved him from his family's
dreams of respectability, as an articled clerk in an insurance office,
but the western desert campaign left him with a permanent touch of
the Yossarians. He was an RAF armourer and really too sensitive
and imaginative for loading bombs on Hudsons. While his mates
daubed vulgar slogans on their bombs Jack would mark his 'Nothing
personal, mate'.

When a dazed Italian wandering across the desert surrendered to
Jack's unit he could not send the man to PoW camp. He fiddled the
paperwork and had the Italian put on the ration strength. The
Italian, now a restaurateur in Florence, stayed with them throughout the campaign. That is why I have been nagging officials of the
Federazione Italiana Golf to take the Italian Open to Florence; Jack
and I had been planning a monumental reunion binge.

On a weekend pass to Cairo, Jack picked up a copy of Fowler's
English Usage and studied it every day of the war, hence his later
reputation of a formidable that-and-which hunter as a sub-editor. On
the golf circuit, he used to break out about once a week and spend the
day in the bar. On these occasions he would march into the press tent
at edition time, plonk himself down at my table and ask: 'What's been
happening?' By long habit he could not read without holding a pencil
in his hand and when he returned my copy it was covered with
grammatical corrections.

That is getting ahead of the story because the reason why Jack
occasionally found life incompatible with a state of complete sobriety
lay back in the desert. The strain of living on a munitions dump
under constant attack, diving into slit trenches and trying to burrow
into the sand, drove him to take refuge in fantasy. He did not want
enemies; he wanted to be friends with everyone.

For the rest of his life, Jack acted out fantasies. He delighted in
walking into a pub and falling into conversation with a stranger. If
the man turned out to be, say, a veteran of the Eighth Army, Jack
would remark that he too had been in the desert and he would salt his
reminiscences with subtle references until his companion realised
that Jack was recalling experiences as a corporal in the Afrika
Korps.

The object of the game was to end up in back-slapping bonhomie
but it did not always work. At a tournament in the north, Jack struck
up a conversation in the bar by correctly surmising that his
neighbour had been a seafaring man. He was in fact a merchant

marine captain who had been sunk by U-boats on three occasions. Jack could not resist the opportunity and said that his brother had been in submarines. 'I remember how proud I felt when his boat came alongside the jetty with the crew mustered on deck and the dawn sun glinting on their leather jackets.' The ex-captain twigged in a flash. 'Leather jackets? It wasn't your brother at all, it was you, you German bastard. That was Bremerhaven!' Jack literally had to run for his life.

Jack's habit of speaking seriously only when he was joking, and vice versa, again backfired when he befriended Eddie Polland. Eddie was then a raw youngster with a pudding basin haircut and a tempestuous migraine temper which caused him to bite lumps out of his golf bag and demolish tee boxes with his driver. Jack realised that the Irish youngster would make terrific copy for the *Sun*. Besides, Polland's vulnerability touched his natural compassion, or what he called his broken-wing syndrome.

What began as a cynical journalistic exploitation of Polland's unsophisticated foibles grew into a genuine friendship, with Jack almost a surrogate father. Polland matured into a fine golfer and Jack into a proud Svengali who inherited Eddie's cast-off sportswear. Jack was fond of announcing the pedigree of his outfits: 'This shirt was third in the Dunlop Masters and these slacks won the Penfold.'

It is customary in saluting the departed to lay on the virtue with a trowel. By conventional standards, Jack had his faults but in 25 years I never knew him harbour a petty thought, or utter a mean word, or commit an act of malice. His brilliant intellect abhorred narrow-mindedness and it was what he considered to be pettifogging insistence on dogma and doctrinal detail which caused him to leave the Roman Catholic church.

As a boy, he had been deeply committed to the church, serving as an altar boy and scrupulously observing his obligations. His one regret was that while his friends were able to confess meaty sins like smoking and groping Children of Mary he was missing out on the gift of Absolution. He earned three plenary indulgences and in a typical moment of generosity in a pub in Blackpool, he bequeathed one of them to me. I just hope that it will be validated because, to go back to the Beatitudes, Jack was the salt of the earth. Life has lost some of its savour.

The Observer, 1982

Henry Howell

Henry Rupert Howell never played in a Walker Cup match and that, on the face of it, remains one of the curiosities of amateur golf.

Being Welsh did not help, for the principality has never indulged in the pressure politics of the Scots and Irish, in pushing their nationals on to the selectors for the sake of chauvinistic kudos. Howell also had thin moustaches in the manner of Ronald Colman and he wore two-tone golf shoes, which was considered to be a barbaric habit or, worse, an American affectation in those snooty days between the wars. Personally I am prepared to give the selectors the benefit of the doubt and accept that they would have overlooked these superficialities, especially in 1932 when Howell beat the national champions of England, Scotland and Ireland on successive days.

By then Howell had emphatically demonstrated that he was one of the best players in the British Isles. But that didn't help. Henry Cotton wrote in his newspaper column at the time: 'We of the professional ranks fail to understand the non-selection of Henry Howell.' Nobody else could understand it either.

The subject of the Walker Cup brings a glint to eyes which first saw the light of day on 23 October, 1899. At his retirement bungalow on the Sussex coast Howell told me: 'In those days the Walker Cup team was chosen from the Oxford and Cambridge Golfing Society, with the odd Scot and Irishman to make up the numbers.'

Incidentally, that 1932 team suffered one of the heaviest defeats in the history of the match, Leonard Crawley winning the only point for the visitors to The Country Club, Brookline, Massachusetts. He also flew the green at the last hole with a two-iron shot, the ball hitting the Walker Cup and putting a dent in it.

It is clear that Howell's face did not fit with the Royal and Ancient Golf Club of St Andrew's and the reason for this mismatch was, equally obviously, the stuffy atmosphere within the closed minds of the selectors.

Howell, you see, was a bit of a card. He made his mark on the game after service as a midshipman on First World War destroyers when he joined the family drapery business in Penarth. He could take time off whenever he wanted it and he had the resources to indulge his zest for the game and for life.

During one Welsh amateur championship at Royal Porthcawl Albert Evans, later president of the Welsh Golf Union, was going down the stairs of his hotel on the way to play Howell and he met his opponent coming up, returning from an all-night binge. The night porter remarked: 'You have a peculiar way of training, Mr Howell.'

Although he was what today would be called a dedicated swinger, Howell was a serious athlete. He went for a daily run before breakfast and practised hard, mostly on his short game. He was an exceptionally straight driver but the real strength of his game was his ability to get down in two strokes from 100 yards. His putting was uncanny.

This touch on and around the greens brought him eight Welsh amateur championships, a plus-three handicap and selection for Wales in 29 home international matches, 20 times as captain, making him by far and away the finest amateur golfer Wales has produced. His skills also gave him the confidence to back himself against the odds and it was this penchant for improving the shining hour with a modest flutter which surely prompted selectorial misgivings. In the Big Room at St Andrew's they debated whether this Welsh chappie was entirely sound.

At Howell's home club, the Glamorganshire at Penarth, his feats have achieved the stature of legend. One of them involves the wager on the number of strokes he would need to play across the course to the furthermost green. Howell covered the best part of a mile in five strokes.

However, his place in golf history was secured forever by an escapade which shines with increasing brilliance in these days of five-hour rounds. The Howell Cup, presented to the Glamorganshire club by his father, is for an important competition in which members must qualify by putting in three cards. Howell had returned two good cards and on the closing date for qualification, a fine June evening in 1926, he was in the bar. Someone asked him if he proposed to put in a third card. He might, he said, if he could find himself a caddie. That problem was easily resolved and the conversation turned to what he felt he might score and how long it would take him to go round.

Howell thought he could score 72 and complete the round in an hour and a half. He was immediately offered odds of 5–1 against such an outcome. He took the bet and others began to offer propositions. How about 6–1 against a 70 in 90 minutes? You're on. And 10–1 against breaking 70 in 75 minutes? Certainly. By now everyone in the bar was suggesting outlandish odds against outlandish combinations. The highest price on offer was 40–1 against an absurd double, 65 in 70 minutes or something of that order. Howell, encouraged by a friend who said he would cover any losses, accommodated them all.

A marker and a timekeeper were appointed and off they went. 'Of course I knew every blade of grass at Penarth and had a clear idea of where I wanted to hit every shot. The course measured about 6,000 yards in those days and I walked quickly between shots. When I went out in 32 I knew I had my chance.'

Howell scored a 63 in 68 minutes and collected on every bet, one of the most remarkable rounds of golf ever played. The amount of his winnings remains his secret, and mine, but it would not cause much of a stir in the bar at Sunningdale, I can tell you.

The Observer, 1985

Bobby Locke

Why Bobby? Well, the nickname was bestowed on Arthur D'Arcy Locke by his African nanny because of his habit of bobbing up and down in his pram. The name stuck with him until the day he died, aged 69 in South Africa last week, although those who followed his remarkable career may have thought it an unseemly style for such an imposing figure.

Walking the fairways in his uniform of white cap, shoes, shirt (invariably with tie neatly tucked below the second button) and blue plus-fours, Locke conveyed the impression of a dignitary taking part in a solemn procession, a bishop at least and possibly even a bishop's butler. The graveside solemnity was most pronounced on the greens where his routine was less a sporting act than the performance of the last rites. Here was an Arthur D'Arcy if ever you saw one.

In fact the stone-faced decorum was a professional pose, the golfer's equivalent of the bedside manner and cultivated for similar reasons. It gave him authority and masked his emotions. Nobody ever knew how Locke was feeling on the golf course but he was alert to every sign of nerves, a muscular twitch or a shortening interval between cigarettes, of his opponents.

Off the course the Bobby fitted him well enough. He was a cheery character, even frivolous, who loved to entertain at parties by accompanying himself on the ukelele as he sang the ditties of the day. He was also exceedingly sentimental, a weakness he would never indulge on the course, and his gratitude for some small kindness could be embarrassingly fulsome.

All his life he thought of himself as British (both his parents were from Ulster), proudly recounted his achievement of being the first Briton to win the Canadian Open since 1914 and fought for Britain as a bomber pilot in the Middle East during the war.

He was besotted by golf almost from the time he was a toddler with a cut-down jigger. Indeed a visiting film crew included footage of the five-year-old golfing prodigy in a documentary which was shown at the Wembley Exhibition of 1923.

South Africa could not contain the growing talents of Locke, who won the South African Open twice as an amateur and, hard though it is to imagine, as a skinny, nine and a half stone amateur at that. He turned pro and his career really took off after the war when he and Peter Thomson of Australia dominated the Open championship. Thomson had the better of that rivalry, with five titles to Locke's four, but Thomson acknowledged that Bobby was the better player, the best in the world for a while.

The Americans laughed at such a suggestion. They did not laugh quite so loudly when Sam Snead visited South Africa for a series of 16 matches against Locke and won only two of them. They sniggered when Locke returned to America with Snead because, by all the sacred laws of golf style, Locke simply could not play.

By now, 1947, Locke was portly and looked a good 10 years older than his years. His swing was a travesty, more of a pirouette than a pivot, with a bent left arm, and it produced a banana shot which started out over the right rough then curved back towards the playing area. How could anyone play like that?

It did not take them long to realise that Locke's looping hook returned the ball to the fairway with monotonous regularity. Nothing seemed to bother this enigmatic man. Even when out-driven by 30 or 40 yards he refused to press, just hitting another round-house shot on to the green.

Then he made their eyes pop. There had been putting specialists before Locke, notably Willie Park Jr and Walter Travis, but in the Forties it was still considered rather eccentric to be obsessive about putting. You either had it or you didn't and there was nothing much you could do about it. Locke had been raised on the most difficult greens in the world and he had analysed the mechanics of the job to the nth degree. By now he had raised putting to an art form and reckoned it a bad day if he took more than 28 putts a round.

He won six tournaments on that first short visit and the laughter turned to muttering. He was later banned from America on a flimsy technicality which hid some unworthy motives.

Locke's fourth Open victory, at St Andrews in 1957, was briefly clouded when an evening television programme after the final round showed that he had marked his ball wide of Thomson's line on the last green and then failed to replace it for his winning tap-in. Locke was in trepidation until he received a letter from N.C. Selway, chairman of the championship committee, which concluded: 'The committee considers that when a competitor has three for the Open championship from 2 feet, and then commits a technical error which brings him no possible advantage, exceptional cirumstances then exist and the decision should be given accordingly in equity and the spirit of the game. Please feel free to show this letter to anyone.'

That letter remained Locke's most treasured possession and as a gesture of humility he privately swore never to wear plus-fours after that day. Like most people, I had assumed that his changed appearance was due to his plus-fours contract having expired. He told me about his vow some little while back over a long and maudlin dinner during which he reflected on his good fortune in having enjoyed such a wonderful life and made so many good friends.

I reminded him that he had suffered his share of rebuffs, insults and hazards along the way and the conversation became quite cheerful as he told slanderous stories about mutual friends who had done him wrong. His last words when we parted were: 'It is a strange thing, master, but in this life there are more horses' asses than there are horses.'

Bobby Locke was from quite the other end of that idiomatic horse.

The Observer, 1987

Guy Wolstenholme

The reason that golf is the best game of them all is that honesty, integrity and sportsmanship are woven into the very fabric of the sport. It is impossible to play golf without them.

In theory it would be possible to achieve the same result by allocating a sharp-eyed referee to every player but that would not be satisfactory, not to say impractical, because so many of the rules hinge on the golfer's intention and the referees would have to be skilled mind-readers.

So golf must be a game of trust. On the whole, golfers are trustworthy and the personal qualities they must bring to the playing of the game carry over into everyday life. Golfers tend to play the ball as it lies whether they are on the course or in the office.

While the game itself imposes these disciplines, the process is enormously helped by the example of individuals. Bobby Jones and Arnold Palmer, among many others, inspired generations of golfers to follow their undeviating lead along the straight and narrow path.

Guy Wolstenholme's name must be recorded high on the list of players whose personal example was a powerful influence for the benefit of golf and the people with whom he came into contact. Sadly, that has to be written in the past tense because Guy died after a typically spirited battle against the one opponent none of us can beat. At least he took the invincible enemy to about six extra holes and he played the game the way it should be played, right to the end.

In the golden age of amateur golf after the war he was one of the outstanding players, with a handicap of plus-four and the only man to get the better of Michael Bonallack in the final of the national championship, the English of 1959, a title he had previously won in 1956.

He also won the Brabazon trophy, played in two Walker Cup matches and two Eisenhower Trophy teams and captured most of the notable amateur titles several times over. When the PGA relaxed its restrictive rule which required amateurs to wait five years after turning pro before qualifying to win prize money, Guy became a pioneer of the movement of gentleman golfers adopting golf as their profession. The word gentleman is used here in its pure sense of a character description although he also qualified for it in its social sense.

The flair which made him such a formidable amateur was not quite so effective in the professional world of grinding out 72-hole stroke play totals but he did well enough, winning the PGA championship and a number of other tournaments. One of them, the Danish Open, was the only national championship I ever entered but I did not resent his success, having missed the cut by a comfortable margin.

Peter Thomson influenced Guy to move to Australia and it says much for his personal qualities that the Aussies accepted the elegant and languid Pom as one of their own. He was a real player and that was all that mattered. The fact that he often warmed up for a round of golf not by playing practice shots but by playing Chopin on the hotel piano was seen as a lovable eccentricity. They called him Schultz, from the strip cartoon, a recondite antipodean joke since

Schroeder is the piano virtuoso, or, more comprehensibly, Tally Ho because of his origins in the hunting shires. Leicestershire, actually. Kirby Muxloe to be precise.

Guy did well in Australia and when he turned 50 in 1981 he was ready to take lucrative advantage of the new Senior Tour in America. He had remarried and had two young sons and a few good years with the seniors would set up the family comfortably.

His play in America in 1982 and 1983 encouraged him to sell up his home in Melbourne and plump for a new life, based on a house he was to have built at Charlotte, North Carolina. The day after the auction of his Australian house he was diagnosed to have cancer.

He made a good recovery from what was described as curative surgery and when we met in Palm Springs for the Vintage Invitational tournament he was in great form, although still weak from his operation, and determined that nothing would prevent him from carrying through his plans. Robyn Wolstenholme, as a nursing sister who had specialised in intensive care, had private reservations about the optimistic prognosis of the surgeons.

Guy played well that week, astonishingly well in the circumstances. It was not until the last day, during one of those interminable airport waits which are an occupational part of professional golf, that he had the first inkling of the cruelty of that expression 'curative' surgery. The brave new life he had planned collapsed.

Knowing and facing the truth, he returned to England to see his family and friends. It was with that knowledge that he saw a sign as he was being driven with his family up the M1: 'Delays possible until October.' 'That won't affect me,' he said, with the dry Wolstenholme humour which his friends had come to know so well. They also knew his courage. Neither deserted him.

Personally, my life was immensely enriched by his friendship and I am sure that the same goes for many, many others. And golf continues to be the best game in the world because of Guy Wolstenholme and his like.

The Observer, 1986

Ronnie Shade

Do any bells ring for you at the mention of David Bell Mitchell? Sadly, the bells have tolled for him and if you have not made the connection already try the initials, D.B.M. That's right, R.D.B.M. Shade, Right Down the Bloody Middle Shade, or Ronnie to his friends, of whom he had rather too many of the fair weather variety towards the end of his life.

It is not necessary to state that he was a tremendous player because the record speaks for itself: Scottish Amateur champion for five years in succession from 1963, three times English amateur stroke-play champion, four times a Walker Cup player, four times a member of the Eisenhower Trophy team.

John Shade, the professional at the Duddingstone club in Edinburgh, was a man of analytical temperament and a perfectionist. He was not interested in golfers who hit fabulous shots some of the time, even most of the time. He wanted to define a method which brought the club-head flush and true to the ball *every* time. Repetitiveness and consistency were his golfing gods and in his son Ronnie, whom he started at golf at the age of two and a half, he had the perfect experimental model for his ideas.

John Shade's ideas had formed gradually after long hours of standing by practice grounds at tournaments watching the great players. Golf, he decided, was essentially geometry and therefore the golfer must perform with the mechanical efficiency of a pair of compasses. Instinct and flair were to be mistrusted because they involved looseness, or mellowness as he called it, and allowed errors to come into the swing.

Ronnie was schooled in the image of his father's geometrical theory, manufactured into a golfer who was so mechanical as to appear almost robotic. The body was to be as steady as a telegraph pole, producing a wooden, rather stiff-legged stance. Now the swing path had to pivot around a point midway between the shoulders and, since the arc had to be identical every time, there must be no play in the joints of the arms. Therefore at the address Ronnie pressed down with his hands, which had the effect of drawing his elbows inwards and creating a rigid triangle of arms and shoulders.

This triangle initiated the take-away, with the hips resisting any tendency to turn and with no rolling of the wrists. Eventually something had to give and the hips had to turn but the legs and lower body continued to resist the rotation of the shoulders, setting up a tension like winding up a spring. Naturally, with such a method, the backswing was short even by the standards of modern professional golf.

The triangle had to be maintained, which meant that there could be no attempt to keep the right upper arm close to the body. The downswing was initiated by a lateral shift and turn of the hips, as far as possible, an exercise which Ronnie used to practise on the tee rather disconcertingly for his opponents.

The downswing looked leisured but, as planned, the contact was invariably solid and the shot right down the bloody middle. You could always recognise Ronnie Shade, if only in silhouette on a distant horizon, by the inordinate time he maintained his focus on the target area after the ball had departed.

That habit of keeping his head down after the strike resulted in a stilted follow through but it was all a part of the doctrine that control was the essence of golf. With such a mechanical method there was a certain loss of length, since the release of the club-head had to be inhibited to a degree, but Ronnie was long enough because he was much straighter than his rivals.

The discipline of the body had to be matched by discipline of the mind and John Shade took Ronnie to tournaments in search of the great players who happened to be out of sorts with their games. They went looking for trouble in order to learn how Bobby Locke, Peter Thomson and John Panton controlled their emotions when things went wrong.

When Ronnie bought a set of clubs in a NAAFI store in Berlin while he was doing his national service and became a force in amateur golf he was expressionless on the course and rigorously suppressed any tendency to gestures of annoyance or delight. You could never tell by looking at him whether he had hit his ball onto the green or into a bunker.

The style of Shade's play produced a predictable pattern of scoring, not many birdies but remarkably few strokes dropped to par. In the World Amateur Team championships in Mexico in 1966 he was over par on only seven of the 72 holes, for a total of 283, on a tough course of 7,125 yards. He missed the fairway from the tee six times, a success rate of 92 per cent which compares with 80 per cent by the most accurate drivers in pro golf today.

The world's greatest golfers find the green in the regulation number of strokes 75 times out of 100. Shade's statistics that week for greens in regulation were 84 per cent. In half of the cases where he did miss the green he chipped and putted for par. With that level of accuracy you would not expect a very low putting average, since hot putting rounds are nearly always the result of missing greens and chipping close, and Shade had an average of 31.5.

Ronnie turned pro at the age of 30 and had early success without ever achieving the level of dominance he had enjoyed in amateur golf. This may have been partly due to his style and competing against men who could make the power game effective but mainly, I believe, because pro golf is mainly a stroke-play game.

Ronnie was the supreme match-player whose consistency ground down his opponents; in one stretch he won 40 matches in succession. He was also one of the good guys, a man without malice or enemies and a good friend. Those seem to be the ones who are singled out for tragedy; Ronnie Right Down the Bloody Middle Shade, on the course and off it, was two years short of his fiftieth birthday when he lost his most important match.

The Observer, 1986

Dai Rees

There was never any doubt about which professional golfer had the Duracell battery. Dai Rees packed about 150 years' worth of living into his three score and ten.

When he was well into his sixties I was recruited as a member of his pro-am team in Bermuda. The heat and humidity parboiled us into a state of torpor which prompted mutinous visions of lounging by the pool with a chinking glass instead of playing golf. Rees promptly shattered that dream. He insisted that his team at least would have no truck with effete electric carts; golf was a walking game. After 36 holes, with Rees darting from rough to rough to instruct each of his troop on how to tackle every shot, golf had become a sweat-soaked, panting, trudging game in the case of us amateurs.

There are about 50 steps up to the Castle Harbour Hotel from the 18th green and, with a cry of 'Last one up buys the beer,' Rees took them at a run, two at a time. His après-golf programme would have exhausted a relay of teenagers.

This dynamism was evident from the earliest days in Barry when the hyperactive toddler had a cut-down baffy put into his hands by his golf pro father. The child became besotted by golf and his parents had to herd him in for meals with a stick. At the age of eight he made a major technical change in his game, discarding the conventional Vardon grip and switching to a two-handed style.

Years later when Rees was appointed professional at Vardon's old club, South Herts, he inherited Vardon's assistant, Steve Thomas, who tried in vain to persuade him back into orthodoxy.

The dominant ingredients of Rees's personality were courage, enthusiasm, generosity and an intensely combative spirit, a recipe more suitable for the hand-to-hand warfare of matchplay than the cold-blooded sniper fire of the card and pencil game. History will judge his record, including three second-place finishes in the Open, as just short of the champion class but, like his compatriot Brian Huggett, matchplay inspired him to world beating standards, especially in national team events.

It was not by fluke or coincidence that Britain's only Ryder Cup victory of the modern era was achieved under Rees's captaincy. That win at Lindrick in 1957 was essentially a personal triumph, because Rees not only demolished his opponents but he managed to instill into his players something of his own battling confidence. His CBE was well-earned.

The game of golf was good to Rees and no player in my experience was more appreciative of his good fortune in being able to indulge the passion of his life as his profession. Requests for him to give talks, or speeches, or clinics for young golfers were welcomed as an opportunity to repay what he felt to be his debt to golf.

He won his first tournament in 1935 and his last 40 years later. David James Rees was short but nobody who knew him could describe him as small, more of a highly concentrated giant.

The Observer, 1983

Henry Cotton

Enthusiasm was the life force of the character and remarkable career of Henry Cotton, who died on Wednesday at the age of 80. It was allied to an ambition of demonic proportions and between them these irresistible forces made him into the greatest golfer in the world while at the same time they came close to destroying him.

When he was barred from the cricket team, his first sporting love, at the Dulwich public school, Alleyn's, because of his refusal to suffer a prefect's caning, he switched his energies to golf. He practised until his hands were raw and his posture became misshapen by the long sessions in the golfer's crouch.

He developed a permanent stomach disorder through gobbling sandwiches instead of pausing for proper meals and every golfer who later came to him for help was lectured seriously on dietary discipline and balanced physical development. 'If you want to be a champion you must live like a champion.'

The dividends from this frenzy of self improvement soon fell due. Cotton won the Open championship of 1934 and repeated that triumph even more impressively three years later in appalling conditions at Carnoustie, a performance as notable for his courage as his skill. Such was his domination of golf at that time that he must have added to those honours but for the war.

He was commissioned into the RAF and while in service he was converted into the Roman Catholic Church after a chance meeting with Fr Peter Blake SJ. His early indiscretions caught up with him and he was invalided out because of abdominal irregularities. So he and his Argentinian wife, Toots, resumed their luxurious life.

Toots was independently wealthy and Cotton commanded unprecedented fees both from the normal business opportunities of golf, including a string of excellent books, but also from such novel ventures as topping the bill in West End variety with a golfing act.

The Cottons moved easily through European society, entertaining and being entertained in the grandest style. This side of his life, the rich fulfilment of his original purpose, probably did more for professional golf than his active campaigning to raise the status of his vocation.

Cotton refused to accept the label of an artisan – when he was forbidden to enter clubhouses he ostentatiously picknicked from a Fortnum's hamper in the back of his Bentley. This cut little ice with his fellow professionals at the time. Mostly they considered him to be an insufferable snob. But his grand house in Eaton Place and his hobnobbing with royalty gave the younger generation of golfers a vision of what could be achieved through golf.

They duly inherited their place in public esteem without, in many cases, the qualifying social graces of their pioneering colleague.

Against the odds, for he was getting on and by no means in good physical shape, Cotton won a third Open, at Muirfield in 1948, and he then channelled his energies into teaching, course design, writing and the good life.

Eventually he and Toots settled at Penina. They loved Portugal and the gentle people of the southern provinces, living in the manner of royalty in exile and cheerfully pleading poverty as they ladled out Beluga caviar to the friends who arrived from every corner of the world to pay homage and play a few holes with the master.

This idyllic existence was interrupted by the Portuguese revolution, when Cotton gave the occupying troops golf lessons until excesses of the hotel's Communist workers' committee became too much to bear.

The Cottons decamped to Spain, taking with them Pacifico, the donkey which never quite mastered the art of caddying with golf bags strapped to its pannier. At Sotogrande the donkey had to be stabled with the polo ponies, all fillies of course. Pacifico died shortly afterwards, from sexual frustration according to Cotton.

Cotton himself nearly died from complications following a fall but when he recovered they were able to return to Portugal. Almost exactly five years ago, on Christmas Day, Toots died and part of Henry died with her.

Cotton used to tell his friends: 'When I die I want to be buried standing up so I can keep an eye on my beautiful Penina.' Now the time has come. The course on which he devoted 20 years of loving development is still as beautiful as ever but Cotton had recently renounced the description 'my' Penina. A change of ownership was followed by changes to his masterpiece.

He was deeply hurt at the time but he was too big a man to allow such a betrayal to get him down for long. His zest for golf carried him through and he even denied himself the luxury of rancour against those who had wronged him, firstly because of his Christian duty but also in order to harness all his emotional strength into creating a new course on the nearby coast where he planned to restate his golfing philosophy.

Others must now complete this new memorial to England's greatest golfer since Harry Vardon and we must hope that they will faithfully interpret his genius.

At this point I must beg indulgence for a personal interpolation.

216

Newspaper obituaries are supposed to be written in advance, dispassionately, on rainy days during the quiet season, and put away in a file. I could never bring myself to anticipate this day. That dereliction was unprofessional and I am conscious now that I have failed to do him justice. For that I am sorry but I am in no frame of mind for dispassionate thought.

There will be no more leisurely nine holes together on the North course, no more convivial dinners, no more mock-horrified shrieks of 'Henry!' from the womenfolk at his ribaldry, no more late-night sessions talking golf, no more scurrilous jokes, no more exchanges of gossip, no more sorties to little fish restaurants in Portimao. Never again will the Post Office have to grapple with the problem of vulgar postcards addressed simply: Dobers, Pratts Bottom, England.

All I really want to say at this moment, and perhaps it is all that really needs saying, is that Henry Cotton was an absolutely bloody wonderful person.

The Observer, 1987

Pat Ward-Thomas

'He has gone where savage indignation can lacerate his breast no more.' Swift would surely not mind sharing his epitaph for he would recognise a soul mate in Pat Ward-Thomas.

There were three Ward-Thomases and the third Ward-Thomas, the golf correspondent of *The Guardian* for more than 20 years, lives on in what he mockingly called his imperishable prose. Newspaper writing is highly perishable but fortunately there are books, including his autobiography *Not Only Golf*.

The other two Ward-Thomases were violently contrasting characters, and both of them entirely different from the gentle, poetic author of his newspaper contributions.

Everyone in golf knew the second Ward-Thomas, the human Vesuvius who looked, in Alistair Cook's description, like a Mexican farmer with 5 acres of beans which weren't doing very well. This volatile persona was assembled when Pat became a journalist after the war and was based on the late Bernard Darwin, the golf correspondent of *The Times*. Darwin was everything Pat conceived a golf correspondent should be; Cambridge Blue and a good enough player to be called out from the press room and take the place of a sick Walker Cup player, winning his match. Darwin was also an elegant essayist: it is a matter of opinion whether he or Neville Cardus should be named as the father of literate sports writing. He also had a hair-trigger temper and a fruity line in self-expression.

Pat's first love was cricket, as a schoolboy fast bowler and with a batting style which prompted the sports master at Wellingborough to describe him as the Wild Man of Borneo. A service commission in the RAF offered him an escape from a dreary job with London Transport and so he was one of the first casualties of the war, the Wellington of which he was co-pilot being knocked out by a German anti-aircraft battery.

The chance discovery of a hickory-shafted woman's mashie in prisoner-of-war camp rekindled Pat's interest in golf and shaped his life. He wrote an account of how the prisoners at Stalag created a camp course and constructed balls from the soles of tennis shoes and soon after the war he resigned his commission for a career in sports writing, hence the reincarnation in the image of Darwin.

He substituted his initials for his Christian name of Percy, assumed the Ward and the hyphen and cultivated the tempestuous Celtic streak in his nature. Perhaps if he had had the chance to open the bowling at Fenner's he might have outgrown his feelings of social inadequacy but that would have robbed his friends of a rich source of amusement for Pat was a snob of Olympic class. Even in reporting golf he would refer to plebeian professionals baldly as Coles or Horton while giving the accolade of Christian name to chaps from decent schools or worthy amateur backgrounds. I never really cracked Pat's code but I think he conferred Christian names after a commoner won a major championship, a bit like giving him his colours.

He was a great walker of golf courses and invariably invited the most socially accepted colleague to accompany him, preferably to watch his adored Arnold Palmer. In my case the walks were infrequent and never lasted long because Pat would soon see someone who was richer, or more celebrated, and he would be off like a heat-seeking missile.

Pat's famous temper could be detonated by the slightest incident, such as the frustration of American hotel breakfasts which required him to unwrap butter pats, pierce milk cartons and open plastic marmalade pots. He was never at his best in the early morning, as evidence his usual embellishment of bits of toilet paper patching the lesions incurred during shaving, and his electrifying roar of 'Damn these bloody parcels' caused waitresses to drop trays and strong men to slop their coffee.

Once embarked on a tirade Pat would warm to his theme, laying about him with increasingly extravagant language until what began as a small mishap with a sugar sachet developed into a wish that the entire blank country should blow itself into oblivion with its own blank bombs.

On these occasions there was only one way of stemming the flow and that was to say firmly: 'Come off it, Pat.' He would then stop in mid blast, grin sheepishly at the absurdity of his artificial anger and the third Pat Ward-Thomas would emerge. His French wife, Jean, could effect this transformation just by saying 'Pat!' rather sharply.

This real, or domestic, Pat Ward-Thomas was a good man, a generous friend and a sensitive writer with a profound appreciation of golf and the beauty of its surroundings. His home club, Royal West Norfolk at Brancaster, represented for him a sanctuary and an inspiration, although it would be an exaggeration to suggest that he invariably found peace on those tranquil links. Things were seldom peaceful for long when Pat had a golf club in his hands.

His period of retirement was sadly brief but in his 68 years he lived with an intensity to cover three lifetimes, relishing his pleasures and his miseries with equal vigour. He was quite a man, all three of him.

The Guardian, 1982